TRIUMPH SINGLES

NITON PUBLISHING

TRIUMPH SINGLES

Late prewar models, Terrier, Cub, Trophy, Blazer and scooters

Roy Bacon

Published by Niton Publishing
P.O. Box 3, Ventnor, Isle of Wight, PO38 2AS

© Copyright Roy Bacon 1991
Reprinted 1997

First published in 1984 in Great Britain by Osprey Publishing Limited,
12-14 Long Acre, London WC2E 9LP
Member company of the George Philip Group

A CIP catalogue record for this book is available
from the British Library

ISBN 1 85579 009 2

Original edition :-
Editor Tim Parker
Design Roger Daniels
Reprinted by Bookbuilders Ltd., Hong Kong

Contents

Edward Turner seated on a Terrier at a dealer launch in Melbourne, a far cry from Meriden

Acknowledgements

This book grew from a thought I had about Cub information. It seemed to me that if I prepared a Cub appendix, as used in other Collector's Library volumes, it would save me much scratching for data when answering my *Classic Bike* agony letters. I mentioned this to Tim Parker (my editor) and was immediately swept up in a wave of enthusiasm to produce a Cub (and Terrier) book. Conversations with friends and booksellers encouraged us to extend our ideas to include at least something on the prewar singles of the late 1930 period and to take in the single cylinder scooters and unit construction, badge engineered, BSA's.

Friends who helped along the way were Don Morley, fellow Collector's series writer, photographer extraordinaire and arch motorcyclist, ever helpful Bob of Blays in Twickenham who put me in touch with Victor of Harwoods in Richmond and my *CB* agony partner, Ken Hallworth who greatly assisted me on the prewar side.

The pictures and line drawings came from various sources. Quite a few, and most of the really old ones, are from the National Motor Museum at Beaulieu who are always so helpful to writers and researchers. It was, therefore, especially pleasant to be able to lend them a few from my own files to add to their archives. The wartime ones are from the Imperial War Museum, another ever helpful source, and other prewar material came from Ken Hallworth.

Many of the pictures came from the files of the magazines and I am again indebted to Peter Law of *Motor Cycle News*, Jim Lindsay of *Mechanics* and Mike Nicks of *Classic Bike* for their help. Ivor Davies, who for so many years was publicity manager at Triumph, kindly raided his photo files to help with some missing shots and most of the line drawings came from the pages of *The Motor Cycle* and *Motor Cycling*.

One picture I can claim as my own but for many of the action ones I have to thank Nick Nicholls and for two of the later ones, Cecil Bailey. Two gentlemen of the camera whose work is always of a high quality. Anthony Smith lent three pictures of his epic journeys and they, plus all the others, were returned after use as usual. Copyright clearance has been sought on all but if I have used an unmarked print, please accept my apologies.

And my thanks to Tim Parker for encouraging an idea into this book.

Roy Bacon
Niton, Isle of Wight
March 1984

This revised edition is published under my *Niton* imprint and includes much additional material sent me by Mike Estall, a great enthusiast for the Terrier and Cub. In particular, he has amplified the notes on numbers, colours and recognition to help all of us know the machines that much better. We are all in his debt.

Mike has all the despatch records for the Terrier and Cub models so can date machines to the day, for which he charges a small fee and issues a certificate. He is keen to receive any further information on the models and, in either case, can be contacted at 24 Main Road, Edingale, Tamworth, Staffs, B79 9HY

Niton, September 1991

1 | Early days for the single

Triumph to most motorcyclists means twins, sometimes triples and models such as the Bonneville, the snarling Tigers or the Trident. Such names were the watchwords for the performance English multi during the postwar era and they dominated the company range and most of its activities. Along a parallel course ran a pair of small singles, the Terrier and the Cub, for which a similar affection was felt by a section of the Triumph buying public and there were enough of them to keep the series in production for a decade and a half.

Triumph singles of the period included the much less popular scooters and, for a brief time in the closing days of the group, a larger machine, created by badge engineering a BSA. Thus, although twins dominated, singles were not forgotten and in earlier times comprised all, or the bulk, of the range. The company, like most others, began its motorcycle life as far back as 1902 with a single.

The firm had its roots in the bicycle industry during Victorian times and was founded by a German, Siegfried Bettmann, in 1885. He began as a factor, selling machines with a Triumph label, but in 1887 was joined by a fellow countryman, Mauritz Schulte, and the following year they established themselves in Coventry to make their own product.

They prospered, expanded and by 1897 had seen the possibilities of power applied to two wheels. To pursue this they imported a

Right above **The first Triumph of 1902 which used a Belgian Minerva engine**

Right **The famous 3½ hp model with the rocking front fork and twin barrel carburettor**

Studio photo of 1909 Triumph with modified forks, tank, rear guard and carrier

Hildebrand and Wolfmüller machine with which to give demonstrations and also looked at the Beeston make. They built a prototype but the matter was not pursued any further.

In 1902 Triumph built their first motorcycle and it was typical of the early Edwardian period. They based it on their standard bicycle which had a Belgian Minerva engine clipped to the down tube from where it drove the rear wheel by direct belt. It was a crude engine with automatic inlet valve and surface carburettor but despite this was imported in quantity and used by many other firms. The cycle parts were also very basic with plain front forks, rim front brake and contracting band rear.

The engine was improved for the next year by the fitting of a mechanical inlet valve and a spray carburettor but was replaced in 1904 by either an English JAP or a slightly larger Belgian Fafnir. A better frame was used for these models and a forecar also built, powered by a water cooled Fafnir, but both the foreign units relied on an automatic inlet valve.

These machines were really only a preamble and in 1905 came the first Triumph engine. This was of 3 hp rating and had mechanical valves operated by internal cam tracks machined into two separate timing gears which meshed with a pinion on the end of the crankshaft. A pair of bellcranks were used to relay the cam form to the valves via tappets set in the crankcase. The engine also had ball bearing mains, a B&B carburettor and, although normally fitted with battery and coil ignition, could be supplied with a magneto. The cycle parts were still based firmly on the bicycle although twin down tubes and strutted, but rigid, front forks were used and these features were not successful.

For the front end Triumph then designed their famous rocking fork with horizontal spring and this was introduced for 1906 together with a stronger frame. From that point the model and the marque became established and known for reliability and sound design. This came at a time when such solidity was needed for the industry, following an initial enthusiasm for motorcycles, tottered through a slump for a year or so. The conservative and successful Triumph design went a long way to ride this period out and played a big part in keeping the infant industry alive.

The company progressed steadily with production increasing from 250 in 1905 to 3000 in 1909. This was helped by the publicity generated from competition success and the firm was among those who ran in the first TT and were rewarded with two places that year and a win in the next TT in 1908. At Brooklands a Triumph won a one lap private match race that year, held two months before the first official event, and the marque went on to many more track successes.

By 1908 the Triumph was fitted with their own design of twin barrel carburettor and attempts were made to provide the rider with something better than a single fixed gear and no clutch. The first offering was a variable pulley but to change the ratio the rider had to stop, screw the pulley in or out and alter the belt length before proceeding. In hilly country this rapidly became tedious and the next option was a Sturmey Archer 3 speed rear hub. This was at first a strengthened cycle component but once engine power rose a stronger and heavier hub became necessary and the resulting weighty rear wheel made the machine most uncomfortable to ride as it fell into potholes. To enable the rider to pull away from a standstill an all metal clutch could be fitted into the rear hub but on the normal touring ratio it was all too easy to let it in too fast and rip out the belt fastener.

It was a problem that beset the industry for

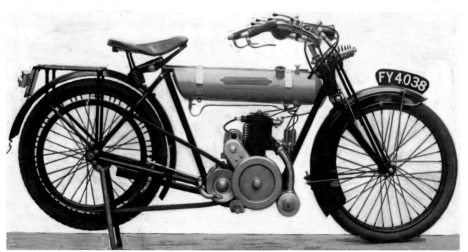

The small two stroke built from 1914 with two speeds, no clutch and ultra-short plug lead

a while as the belt was so cheap and quiet but in the end the separate gear box with clutch had to come but not for some years on a Triumph. In 1910 they did double the range and produced two models, one a sporting TT machine with a short wheelbase frame, no pedals and equipped either for the road or racing. The second was a tourer, longer, with pedals and with the option of the hub clutch.

At this their design stagnated until 1914 when a new machine was launched. This had a small 225 cc two stroke engine plus a two-speed gearbox worked by a lever mounted on the bars and connected to the box by cable. No clutch was fitted so gear changing required a delicate touch if violent results were to be avoided. Engine and gearbox were mounted close together with the magneto behind the first and over the second. As the plug was screwed into the rear of the one-piece, all horizontally finned, head and barrel the plug lead was thought to be the world's shortest. Cycle parts copied the larger model with rocking fork, rim front and belt rim rear brakes plus the traditional light grey finish with red lined, green panels. It was called the Junior model by the firm but nicknamed 'the Baby' by the public.

Early in 1915 it was joined by the famous model H which was based on the older 500 cc engine but with revised timing gear and other improvements. This drove by chain to a three-speed Sturmey Archer gearbox with clutch and kickstarter although the final drive remained by belt. The rocking front fork was fitted along with the stirrup front brake and the model went to war to the tune of 30,000 machines supplied to the army. It enhanced the sobriquet 'Trusty', used in Triumph advertising for several years prior to the Great War.

When the war ended the men came home and demanded transport for they had learnt of its benefits and of things mechanical. A young man's gratuity might not stretch to a car but a motorcycle was something else and there was a boom in sales. This was smaller than it should

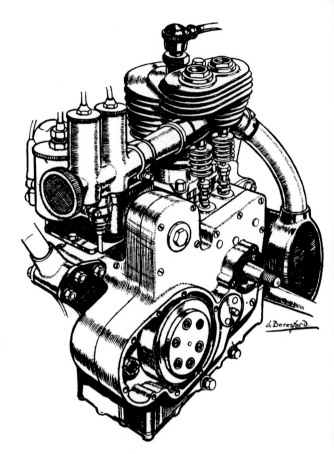

Above **The unit construction 350 cc model LS of 1923 with overhung crankshaft**

Right **The 4 valve Ricardo Triumph in 1925 with Druid forks and drum front brake**

have been due to iron foundry strikes in 1919 which restricted production and then massive inflation which pushed prices up and out of reach. Within a year or two the boom was over, prices fell and cash was short so the industry was back on hard times.

At Triumph they were able to get back into production faster than most by simply demobilising the model H into its civilian finish. With that underway it was easy enough to expand the line with the model D, a single gear version of the H, the 500 cc TT model and the small Junior but the use of belt drive could not continue for much longer and in 1920 came all chain drive.

The model was the SD which used the H engine in a new frame complete with sidecar lugs. It had a 3 speed Triumph gearbox with cross-over drive so the rear chain went on the right and the clutch incorporated a transmission shock absorber. A kickstarter was fitted but for all the advance in transmission the remainder of the machine stayed old fashioned with its rocking fork and rim brakes.

Aboard an enlarged 269 cc version of the Junior was built under licence and sold in the USA for a year or so and in Germany for longer. The German connection dated back to 1903 and was to continue until 1929 when Triumph-Werke Nürnberg, or TWN as they became known, went their own way.

In 1921 Triumph took one big step forward to produce a new engine that not only had ohv but also a 4 valve head. This was their model R which had the top half designed by Harry Ricardo, so enthusiasts shortened the name to Riccy just as a later generation would call their Triumph twin the Bonnie. In truth the machine was the SD below the crankcase mouth but above that went a steel barrel with machined fins and the cast iron head. The combustion chamber was in penthouse roof form with each pair of valves parallel and the pairs set at 90 degrees to each other. The pushrods were exposed and the rockers pivoted on ball races while, although the single carburettor fed into a common manifold, each exhaust port connected to a pipe that ran to a silencer box across the front of he engine.

At first the rocking fork was used but at the TT these were changed for Druids with side springs which were an inprovement even if nothing special. In the race the Ricardo models had problems while a side valve TT machine set the fastest lap but the next year a Ricardo took a fine second place. The same year, 1922, saw the production model R reaching the showrooms with an iron cylinder and other detail changes. For the rest the public continued to be

offered the traditional H, SD and Junior models much as before.

1923 saw the two stroke enlarged to 250 cc while the model also gained a clutch and a gear lever although it retained both the rocking fork and belt drive to the end late in 1925. Of more technical interest was the LS which had a surprising specification for a model coming from a firm that still used belt drive. It had a unit construction engine and gearbox with gear primary drive and was powered by a 350 cc side valve unit.

The engine and gearbox made a neat unit with a run of gears on the right to connect the crankcase with the timing gears, magneto and clutch. The gearbox contained 3 speeds with the chain final drive on the left and the box end cover

extended forward to form a door to the crankcase. Behind this lay an overhung crankshaft, an unusual feature on a four stroke, and below the engine went the sump for the oil which was fed under pressure to the bearings by a plunger pump. On the cycle side there were Druid forks and at last a drum front brake which also went onto the Ricardo model.

The model ran on through 1924 but with the industrial unrest of the times sales were low, so Triumph decided to go for a really simple, rugged machine at the lowest of prices and thus offer Ford model T type motorcycling to the public. The aim was to get real production quantities of a prosaic design by paring it to the bone and the result was the model P. It hit rock bottom

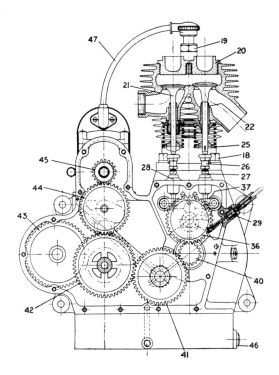

Above **LS model gear train, up to camshaft, back via idler to clutch and gearbox, then up again to magneto**

Left **The engine of the Ricardo with single carburettor and horizontal sparking plug**

in price and penny pinching and sold at a figure well below that of any other 500 then on the market. To do this it used one or two features that really did go beyond the bounds of decent cost cutting and one such was a virtually useless front brake. The open roads of the times and the low price made amends for this and other faults.

For all that, it sold and in 1925 that was what mattered. It gave the owner a solid side valve engine, 3 speeds and a chain drive so it was not surprising that production soared to 1000 machines a week. Late that year the first 20,000 had been built and Triumph rectified the front brake and improved the big end, clutch release and valve guides before the second batch began to roll.

Alongside the P ran the R, SD and LS models and for 1927 they were joined by others. Two were related to the P, the N having a heavier frame and the Q more polish, but the W was new with the odd capacity of 277 cc in an endeavour to give as much engine as possible while keeping below a 220 lb tax limit weight. Also new was a 2 valve TT model based on the machine raced at Brooklands by Vic Horsman and this had dry sump lubrication, saddle tank and much of the style of the thirties. It was to replace the Ricardo which had continued without development but went at the end of the year.

The company was then engaged in introducing a new small car and found itself hard pressed to cope so the 1928 range was much reduced. The W continued as did the new TT model while the P became the NP and was joined by the N de luxe with a new frame and saddle tank. At the same time the old grey and green tank finish was replaced by a new one in black with blue panels carrying a globe transfer.

By 1929 production matters at the works were sorted so the motorcycle range was enlarged again with a trio of models using many common engine parts. There were the 350 cc ohv CO, 500 cc sv CN and a heavy duty 550 cc sv CSD which all had saddle tanks as did the NP and N de luxe. The W continued without this aid to styling but was joined by the WS which was fitted with one at extra cost. The sports 500 changed its typing to the model ST and was fitted with the new form of tank and a new frame to lower the riding position.

It was a good year to end the decade but then the effects of the depression began to bite hard. For 1930 Triumph, like many others, followed the trend for inclined engines and built a whole range from 250 to 550 cc with dry sump lubrication and the oil carried in an extension of the crankcase. On a couple of models steel pressings covered all the crankcase and gearbox, said to be for neatness and style despite the reduced

TRIUMPH 1.47 h.p. O.H.V. - - - Model 'XO'

SPECIFICATION :

ENGINE : 1.47 h.p. inclined single cylinder, 56.6 × 59 mm. bore and stroke, detachable hemispherical head, engine torque member, overhead valves, enclosed rockers and adjustable pushrods, oval aluminium piston. Dry sump lubrication, adjustable force feed to roller bearing big end and silent harmonic cam gears. IGNITION : Dynamo and coil, extremely accessible. SILENCING : Large silencer box, fishtail outlet. TRANSMISSION : Non-metallic shock absorber in rear wheel. Hand controlled clutch. Three speed gear with hand control. FRAME : Duplex pattern, low saddle position, welded steel tank, capacity 2¼ gallons. STEERING : Triumph forks with single tension spring. CONTROLS : Triumph integral clean handlebar, adjustable sports pattern, enclosed cables. WHEELS : Dunlop tyres 25 ins. × 3.00 ins., internal expanding brakes. PROTECTION : Generous leg-shields. EQUIPMENT : Electric lighting with ignition warning light and switch integral with headlamp, strong metal tool box, knee grips, lifting handle (carrier optional). FINISH : Frame coslettised and enamelled black. Tank distinctively panelled. All bright parts chromium plated.

Price (for Great Britain and Northern Ireland) XO, complete with electric lighting (Tax 15/-) **£28 10s.** or **£7 8s. 9d.** down and 12 monthly payments of **£2 4s. 3d.**

TRIUMPH 5.49 h.p. Model 'ND'

5.49 h.p. inclined engine 84 × 99 mm. bore and stroke enclosed side-by-side valves, aluminium piston. Dry sump lubrication, force feed to roller bearing big end and cam gear. Efficient silencer. Non-metallic shock absorber. Hand controlled clutch. Three speed gear with hand control. Crankcase and gearbox shield. Low saddle position. 2¼ gallon saddle tank, Triumph clean handlebar, integral levers, enclosed cables. Dunlop Tyres 26 × 3.25 ins., internal expanding brakes. Complete kit of tools. Frame coslettised and enamelled black. Tank distinctively panelled. All bright parts chromium plated.

Prices (for Great Britain and Northern Ireland) ND.1 without Lamp or Horn **£45** or **£11 6s. 2d.** down and 12 monthly payments of **£3 11s.**

TRIUMPH 4.93 h.p. O.H.V. Model 'NT'

Same specification as above but fitted with 2-port overhead valve engine. 84 × 89 mm. bore and stroke capacity 493 c.c. Chromium plated tank.
NT.1 without Lamp or Horn **£46** or **£11 19s. 6d.** down and 12 monthly payments of **£3 11s. 8d.**

For Prices of Electric Lighting and Instrument Panel equipment, etc., see back of folder.

One page from the 1932 catalogue showing the new 150 fitted with tension spring forks

TRIUMPH 2.49 h.p. O.H.V. - - - Model 'WO'

SPECIFICATION :

ENGINE : 2.49 h.p. inclined single cylinder, 63 × 80 mm. bore and stroke, capacity 249 c.c., detachable 2-port hemispherical head, engine torque member, overhead valves, roller bearing rocker operation, enclosed adjustable pushrods, oval aluminium piston. Dry sump lubrication, adjustable force feed to roller bearing big end and cam gears. IGNITION : High tension magneto. SILENCING : Two large silencer boxes with anti-drumming device. TRANSMISSION : Non-metallic shock absorber in rear wheel. Hand controlled clutch. Three speed gears with hand control. FRAME : Straight tubular type, easily detachable crankcase and gearbox shield, low saddle position, saddle tank with rubber bush mounting at forward end, capacity 2 gallons. STEERING : Triumph forks with single tension spring : Adjustable handlebar, ignition and throttle twist grips, integral levers, enclosed cables. WHEELS : Dunlop tyres 25 ins. × 3.00 ins. internal expanding brakes. EQUIPMENT : Strong metal tool box, knee grips, lifting handle (carrier optional). FINISH : Frame coslettised and enamelled black. Tank and all bright parts chromium plated.
Prices (for Great Britain and Northern Ireland) W.O.1 without Lamp or Horn (Tax 30/-) **£36 10s.** or **£9 3s. 9d.** down and 12 monthly payments of **£2 18s. 2d.**

For Prices of Electric Lighting and Instrument Panel equipment, etc., see back of folder.

TRIUMPH " 500 " COMPETITION O.H.V. Model 'CD'
(With 4-Speed Gear)

4.93 h.p. inclined engine, 84 × 89 mm. bore and stroke, 2-port, overhead valves, roller bearing rocker operation, aluminium piston, polished and ground ports. Dry sump lubrication, force feed to roller bearing big end and cam gear. Two upswept silencer pipes with large expansion boxes. Non-metallic shock absorber. Hand controlled clutch. Four speed gear with foot control. Low saddle position, 2½ gallon saddle tank. Sports pattern handlebar with external controls (Triumph clean pattern handlebar optional). Dunlop tyres 27 × 2.75 ins., front, 26 × 3.25 ins., rear, internal expanding brakes. Complete kit of tools. Frame coslettised and enamelled black. Tank and all bright parts chromium plated.

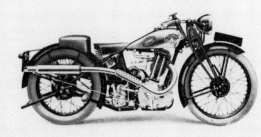

Price (for Great Britain and Northern Ireland) CD.1 without Lamp or Horn **£47** or **£11 15s. 6d.** down and 12 monthly payments of **£3 13s. 9d.**

For Prices of Electric Lighting and Instrument Panel equipment, etc., see back of folder.

The specifications and prices printed in this folder are subject to alteration without notice.

Another 1932 page giving details of the WO with enclosed nether regions and the exposed CD access, but more to reduce costly polishing of cast alloy parts.

This range, some with twin port engines, was joined by the model X which had a neat 175 cc two stroke engine built in unit with a 2 speed gearbox all mounted in a duplex frame. In the effort to find customers there were more changes for 1931 with the two stroke reduced to 150 cc and joined by a pair of competition models and another pair called Silent Scouts. These were aimed at the sophisticated rider who wanted weather protection and quiet running. To give this, extensive panels enclosed the engine and formed legshields, while the second requirement was met with special cam forms.

The depressed industry was helped a little for 1933 with the introduction of a cheap machine tax for under 150 cc machines. Triumph joined the rush to the Villiers works for 98 and 150 cc units which went into machines sold under the Gloria label at rock bottom prices. In addition they produced a very nice ohv unit of 150 cc with inclined cylinder and coil ignition which they fitted into the X frame to make the XO.

In 1932 they were fortunate enough to gain the services of Val Page who joined them from Ariel where had been working since 1925. Page was quiet, modest, a gentleman and a brilliant engineer who saw that the hard times called for well designed motorcycles without frills or gimmicks. Cheapness, reliability, simple construction and easy maintenance were what was needed and he set to work to provide these features in a range of singles that were to carry the firm to the end of the decade and through the war. He also designed a 650 cc twin, mainly for sidecar use, to top the range but this was less successful.

His single range ran from 250 to 500 cc with side and overhead valve engines offered in touring and performance versions. The only model to continue from the old collection was the 150 which retained its sloping engine as the X05/1 and was joined by a 175 cc version, the X07/1.

All the ohv models, including the two small slopers, were offered in a /5 guise with high compression piston, hotter cams and polished ports for the sporting rider but the bulk of production was of the basic motorcycles with prosaic appearance and performance.

The Page machines were very English in their conception and execution. Each engine was based on a built-up crankshaft with massive flywheels fitted with separate mainshafts held on a keyed taper by a substantial nut. The big-end was a double row, uncaged roller running on a crankpin pulled up in tapered holes by nuts. The connecting rod carried a hardened sleeve in its lower end for the big end rollers and a bush at the top for the gudgeon pin.

The piston with its three rings ran in an iron barrel and the side valve had the valve chamber cast into the side. The overhead one only needed clearance for the pushrod tubes and in both cases the barrel sat on studs in the crankcase. The side valve head was a simple cover to carry the plug and sealed to the barrel with a gasket but on the ohv engines a ground joint was used. The iron head carried each valve in a well and was surmounted by an alloy rocker box. This was in two parts and split on the rocker centre line with the pushrod tubes sealing to the underside. The lid carried the valve lifter and a plate on the right connected the rocker spindles to the cylinder head.

The crankcase was split on the engine centre line and cast in aluminium with a detachable sump plate and gauze filter. The right case extended back to form the timing chest and also had a platform to carry the magneto. Each camshaft was gear driven from the crankshaft and moved a tappet, in a guide pressed into the crankcase, and a pushrod. Valve clearance was set with adjusters at the top of the tappets for both side and ohv engines. The timing gear train used an idler which drove the mag-dyno gear. This was held to the shaft taper by a nut and the fixing embodied an extractor device.

TRIUMPH "SILENT SCOUT" 4.93 h.p. O.H.V. Model 'B'
(With 4-Speed Gear)

SPECIFICATION :

ENGINE : 4.93 h.p. inclined single cylinder, 84 × 89 mm. bore and stroke, capacity 493 c.c., detachable 2-port hemispherical head, engine torque member, overhead valves, enclosed roller bearing rockers, adjustable push rods, oval aluminium piston. Dry sump lubrication, adjustable force feed to roller bearing big end and silent harmonic cam gears. IGNITION : High tension gear driven magneto. SILENCING : Two large silencer boxes, fishtail outlet. TRANSMISSION : Non-metallic shock absorber in rear wheel, primary drive enclosed in oil bath case. Hand controlled clutch. Four speed gears with hand control. FRAME : Straight tubular type, low saddle position, saddle tank mounted on rubber bushes at rear end. STEERING : Triumph forks with single compression spring. CONTROLS : Adjustable handlebar, ignition and throttle twist grips, integral levers enclosed cables. WHEELS : Dunlop Tyres 26 ins. × 3.25 ins., internal expanding brakes. EQUIPMENT : Strong metal tool box, knee grips, lifting handle (carrier optional). FINISH : Frame coslettised and enamelled black. Tank and all bright parts chromium plated.

Price (for Great Britain and Northern Ireland) B.1 without Lamp or Horn **£51 10s.** or **£13 16s.** down and 12 monthly payments of **£3 18s. 4d.**

For Prices of Electric Lighting and Instrument Panel equipment, etc., see back of folder.

TRIUMPH "SILENT SCOUT"
5.49 h.p. ———— Model 'A'
(With 4-Speed Gear)

Same specification as Model B. but fitted with side valve engine, 5.49 h.p. 84 × 99 mm. bore and stroke, capacity 548.5 c.c. and one large silencer.

Price (for Great Britain and Northern Ireland) A.1 without Lamp and Horn **£49 10s.** or **£12 13s. 6d.** down and 12 monthly payments of **£3 16s. 8d.**

For Prices of Electric lighting and Instrument Panel equipment, etc., see back of folder.

And yet again from 1932, a page of Silent Scouts with harmonic cam forms and big silencers

The entire timing side was enclosed by a single cover which had an access screw in line with the magneto nut to allow the ignition timing to be set without disturbing the cover. The exhaust camshaft extended through the cover and had an offset pin machined into its end. This drove a double plunger oil pump via a sliding block and the pump was bolted in place and then enclosed by its own small round cover. The lubrication system was dry sump with a pressure feed to the big end and the oil was kept in a tank mounted on the right beneath the saddle.

A cam type shock absorber on the left end of the crankshaft drove a 4-speed gearbox by chain. Most of the Page machines had foot-change and the transmission was conventional with the output sleeve gear concentric with the mainshaft and the layshaft below with the kick-start quadrant meshed with a ratchet gear on the mainshaft.

The remainder of the machine was normal for the times so the frame was rigid and built up from tubes brazed into lugs. At the front went girder forks with a central barrel spring and friction dampers built into the front, upper pivot. A steering damper was also supplied with the friction discs below the bottom crown brought into play by a knob above.

Both hubs were equipped with good sized single leading shoe brakes and the front backplate carried a speedometer drive gearbox whose pinion meshed with the hub. At the rear the drum was on the sprocket side with a direct rod to the brake pedal and pressed steel guards protected both front and rear chains.

Equipment was to the period with a saddle for the rider and a rear stand for parking. The battery went on the left to match the oil tank and a toolbox went to the rear on the right. Some models had twin port heads and so were fitted with two exhaust systems, these could be upswept in the sports fashion of the era.

The machines may have lacked real style but they were solidly built and reliable so sold well.

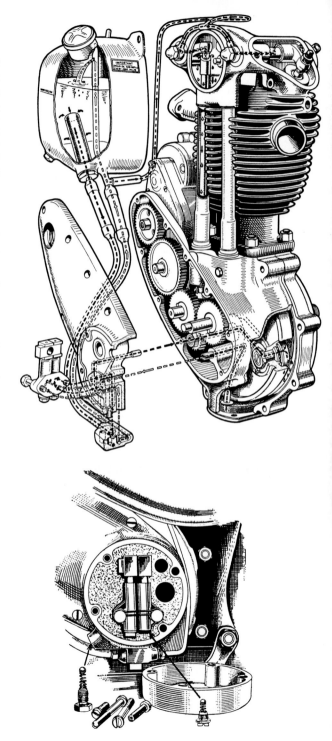

Above **A 1937 model 3H pictured in 1982, a stalwart single in peace and war**

Left above **The prewar single in its 3HW military form. Gears were favoured for the timing chest at Triumphs**

Left **The famous twin plunger oil pump driven by the exhaust camshaft**

They seemed set fair to carry the firm on for a good run but late in 1935 Triumph found itself in deep financial water as it had over-extended itself on the car side. For a while it seemed that the Coventry motorcycle had reached the end of the road but fortunately rescue was at hand.

The man who brought this about was Jack Sangster who was no stranger to two wheels as his family had been in control at Ariel from Victorian times. He heard that Triumph were in trouble and after some hard bargaining became the new owner of the motorcycle business which split completely from the car side of the company.

To run Triumph he chose Edward Turner whom his father, Charles, had taken onto the Ariel staff in 1929 to develop his ideas of a square four engine under Val Page. This design had become the top Ariel model and when Page went to Triumph Turner had become chief designer. He had a motorcycling background having run a small repair business in London and during this period designed and built a machine fitted with a 350 cc overhead camshaft engine.

By all accounts he was a hard man to work for, often demanding the impossible from his staff, and getting it, so there were stormy scenes at Triumph on occasion. For all his difficult ways he saw very clearly the need to keep costs within bounds and he turned Triumph into a very efficient unit with a minimum of non-productive people on the payroll. Many of the staff fulfilled several functions, there was no empire building, impossible with a dictator, and the firm was very profitable.

One of those to move on was Val Page who joined BSA to draw up their dry sump range and for them he moved the oil pump right down into the sump and made it a gear unit. In other respects it was an updated repeat of his Ariel and Triumph work taken on to use the best points from each. In 1939 he returned to Ariel while Turner spent a few of the war years at the BSA plant.

Above **Engine and primary chaincase of the 1937 model 3H**

Left **Model 3/1, the 350 cc side valve machine, at rest on an airfield. Early gearbox so most likely this was a conscript swept up early in the war** (*IWM*)

Edward Turner was a designer who made the metal work by keeping the weight down at the drawing board stage. If anything broke on test it was strengthened, otherwise it remained as it was and this made for light machines with a good performance. His real flair was however his sense for feeling the public's buying pulse and for adding a cosmetic touch that would ring the sales bell with them. He did this first with the Ariel Red Hunter and for 1936 repeated the exercise with the Triumph single.

By then the XO models had gone and from the sports models he created the Tiger series by adding chrome plated tanks with silver sheen panels and a bright sparkle to other parts. It made all the difference and the new names were a touch of genius. They came in 250, 350 and 500 cc sizes labelled Tiger 70, 80, or 90 with the number suggesting the machine top speed.

For 1937 the Tigers received a new and nicer tank shape, shared with other models in the range, and upswept exhaust pipes, polished timing cases, a cast alloy chaincase, also polished and a good few minor parts with a chrome finish. It gave them a real sparkle, even if the lines were so like those of the Red Hunter, and the customers loved them. For the remainder of the decade they sold well backed by the other singles in their more sober livery.

When war broke out in 1939 all machines held as stock were impounded so at first the forces had an array of models to ride. Quickly this situation was simplified with each firm producing one or two models of the same basic type to keep the spares holding simple. For Triumph the choice was a pair of 350s, one with side and the other with overhead valves although in the early days of the war Triumph also supplied some 500 cc side valve machines.

In company with other firms they set out to meet a ministry specification for a single machine for all forces. The prize for success was high for the chosen model would be built by all to the benefit of the originator. Triumph designed a very light 350 cc twin which proved to be the best answer and the intention was to proceed with it. This was brought to nought late in 1940 when the factory was bombed and in the grim days that followed production was the only thing that mattered so the new design was put aside.

Triumph lived in temporary quarters for a while but by 1942 had managed to find a new site at Meriden and installed some machinery. Despite the loss of the factory and the move they built very nearly 50,000 motorcycles during the war years plus a host of other items. The best known of these was the generator set used by the RAF from which came the alloy head and barrel of the postwar Grand Prix and Trophy models.

The main wartime model was the 350 cc ohv developed from the Tiger 80 and typed the 3HW. Due to a shortage of aluminium the cylinder head was modified so the rocker boxes were cast in one with it in iron and this technique was used postwar for the same capacity twin.

At the end of the war Triumph considered producing a civilian version of the 3HW in black and this project reached the point of a leaflet being produced to describe it. In the end the demand for twins was so great that it took all the production capacity and there was no point in building the less profitable single. It would also have been awkward to make alongside the twins and in fact, in time, Triumph were to drop their early 350 twin for similar reasons.

A good many of the service machines did reach the public after the war when the surplus stock was sold off. The models were brought up in batches by enterprising dealers who gave them a respray, usually in maroon or black, and sold them to transport hungry riders. Later on many of these machines were tuned up and at weekends battled it out on grass, road or scrambles circuit where alcohol fuel made the all-iron engine no handicap.

After the war, in 1945, it was twins only in the Triumph range and neither singles nor side valves

although they did build a twin in that form for the services. For some time the government was crying for exports while riders craved machines so the factory concentrated on its profitable twins. It was not until the early fifties that they returned to the single and when they did it was a model for a different market but once more a Triumph success.

Left **Stripping the gearbox of a 3HW. Note the air cleaner on the tank top for desert use** (*IWM*)

Below **A Tiger 70 pictured at Goodwood in 1983. In the early postwar years many of these models were used for road racing, grass track, scrambles and sprints with success**

2 | Terrier and Cub

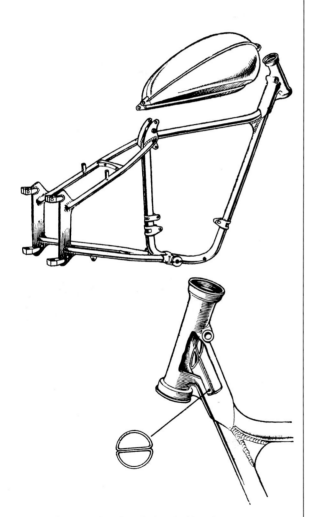

Terrier frame and tank with detail of headstock area construction

In November 1952 a new Triumph single was announced just in time to take its place among the twins at the Earls Court show. It represented a change of ideas for the firm and a return to the commuter market they had supplied before the war. Then they had used 250 cc but for the new machine decided that a good 150 would provide the necessary performance.

Edward Turner declared early on that the new model had to out-perform its rivals and look like a Triumph. He also wanted it to have sparkle so that youngsters would buy one, like the marque and in due course move on to a twin. A ploy that has always worked, was forgotten in later years by the group and rediscovered by the Japanese.

The new model was called the Terrier and appeared among a sea of prosaic 125s using Villiers engines. Nearly all these were cheap in price, design and quality with only the Bantam and Enfield Flea standing out as exceptions. Turner spurned the idea of a cheap motorcycle, he offered instead a low price machine which was not at all the same thing. This was done by making the metal work and keeping factory efficiency high.

He chose a four-stroke because at that time it gave more power and it avoided the dilemma of either using a Villiers power plant and joining the herd, or going into the two-stroke design field. He maintained that the cost difference was small and even if his machine cost more, it would have more rider features, copied from the twins, to compensate. Lower fuel consumption and no petroil would offset any difference in a year's running and Turner stated that he preferred green oil to slightly coloured petrol for two-stroke lubrication.

So the new Triumph was a lightweight built in the Triumph image with a unit construction engine the single cylinder of which inclined forward 25 degrees nearly parallel to the frame down tube. It had a four-speed gearbox, an alternator, coil ignition and plunger rear suspension. The styling was taken from the twins with headlamp nacelle, tank badge bars and clean handlebar line while the finish was the traditional amaranth red. It was truly another Triumph baby.

For his new single Turner made the bore and stroke near equal to keep the unit compact and this decision allowed the use of generous valve sizes. Actual dimensions were 57 × 58·5 mm and the capacity was 149 cc. Compression ratio was 7·0:1 and power output 8·3 bhp at 6500 rpm.

The engine construction was unusual, for the crankcase was not split on the vertical centre line but instead was split to the left of the crankshaft. Once this item was installed a door, carrying the drive side main, was fitted to complete its support and this extended to the rear to form the inner primary chaincase. This reduced the number of castings and gave a rigid assembly.

The crankshaft itself was built up by pressing each cast iron flywheel onto the case hardened steel crankpin. On the timing side the mainshaft was integral with the wheel and its length was kept low to aid assembly and maintain its strength. The longer and more highly stressed drive side shaft was in the same steel as the crankpin and a press fit into the flywheel. A serrated flange stopped it turning in the wheel.

The big end bearing was a single row of rollers running in the forged steel connecting rod. This was bushed for the gudgeon pin which carried a piston fitted with one oil and two compression rings and was retained on the pin by circlips. It

Above **The Terrier engine in its first form with points housing behind cylinder**

Right **Front page advert showing the trim Triumph lines to advantage**

ran in a cast iron barrel that was deeply spigoted into the crankcase and was finished with aluminium paint to match the rest of the engine. This was not the ideal technical colour but the barrel was well finned and uniform in section so its cooling was adequate. An alloy barrel was considered an unnecessary complication which would have put up costs with no real advantage in cooling or weight.

The cylinder was also spigoted up into the light alloy head with a gasket between the two. Four long studs screwed into the crankcase and with four sleeve nuts at the top held both items in place. The head and rocker box were formed in

7 MAY 1953   EVERY THURSDAY EIGHTPENCE

THE MOTOR CYCLE

FOUNDED 1903 · CIRCULATES THROUGHOUT THE WORLD

A Real TRIUMPH – *in Miniature!*

THE

TRIUMPH Terrier

| 150 c.c. O.H.V. | UNIT CONSTRUCTION ENGINE/GEARBOX | 4 SPEED FOOT OPERATED GEARBOX | TELESCOPIC FORKS AND SPRING FRAME |

TRIUMPH ENGINEERING CO. LTD., MERIDEN WORKS, ALLESLEY COVENTRY

November 12, 1953.

MOTOR CYCLING

TRIUMPH

presents the

200 c.c. TIGER CUB

Bred in the tradition of the famous Triumph "Tigers," the new 200 c.c. "Tiger Cub" will appeal instantly to all lovers of sporting lightweights. With a high efficiency overhead valve engine, dry sump lubrication, unit construction four-speed gearbox and spring frame, its specification includes all the accepted best features of a big motorcycle. Also, like the new "Tigers" 100 and 110, it is finished in shell blue sheen and black. See this striking new addition to the Triumph range on the Triumph stand (No. 34) at Earls Court. Specification folder on request.

THE BEST MOTORCYCLE IN THE WORLD

TRIUMPH ENGINEERING CO. LTD., MERIDEN WORKS, ALLESLEY, COVENTRY

Above **Cable operated, digital gear indicator**

Left **Full page advert for the Cub showing its raised exhaust and the massive period rectifier beneath the seat**

Below **Oil system used by Terrier and Cub**

one with the fins above the head set in a chevron pattern to encourage air flow in the desired directions. The valve seats were machined to a dovetail to secure them into place once the head was cast round them.

The exhaust port was a steel sleeve while the inlet passage terminated at its outer end in a flange and two studs to carry the small Amal type 332 carburettor with its separate float chamber. Each end of the rocker box carried a single spindle on which oscillated a rocker with an adjuster at its outer end. A dished cover closed off each box and was retained by a single locknut on a stud. Each valve was closed by duplex springs held by a collar and split collets and moved in a cast iron guide which had a circlip to locate it.

The timing gear was the simplest with a pinion on the crankshaft driving a gear on the end of the camshaft above it. This ran in bushes and each cam lifted a hardened steel tappet which ran direct in the crankcase. The inner cam was

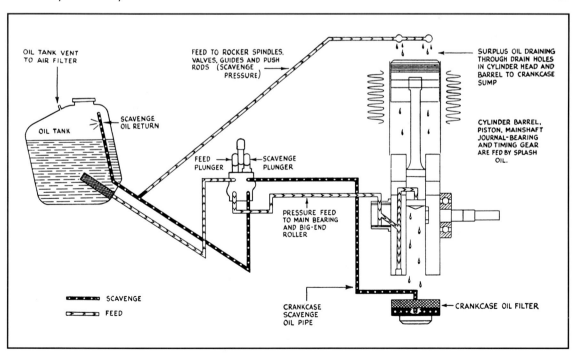

the exhaust and the outer the inlet and each tappet lifted a pushrod which had a hardened end cap at the top only. At the bottom the rod sat in a depression in the tappet top and the pair of rods were enclosed by a plated tube which sealed to the crankcase and the underside of the rocker box.

The crankshaft pinion was unusual in that it was made with a male taper that fitted into the end of the mainshaft to which it was located by a pin and held by a bolt. A skew gear was machined inboard of the timing pinion and drove a vertical shaft situated aft of the crankshaft and this was connected to two items. The lower end of the shaft was machined with an offset pin and this was coupled by a short rod to a twin plunger oil pump. The pump plungers were thus parallel to the ground and the assembly was located on a mounting face in a compartment below the timing gears.

The pump was supplied from an external tank which contained a filter and the oil was forced into the crankshaft via the timing side main bearing bush. Drillways fed the bush and the oil then entered the shaft for a further series of holes to deliver it to the crankpin. The remainder of the engine's lower half and the piston relied on splash lubrication but the rockers were supplied by a take off from the return line. Engine breathing was looked after by a timed port in the outer camshaft bearing and a second filter was fitted in the base of the crankcase from where the oil was scavenged.

The vertical shaft also drove a distributor unit which housed the contact points for the coil ignition and the centrifugal advance mechanism for their cam. The whole assembly could be rotated to set the timing and tucked in out of the way very nicely.

The main crankcase casting was in aluminium

Exploded drawing of the Terrier engine around 1954. Plain big end and timing side main were used for many years

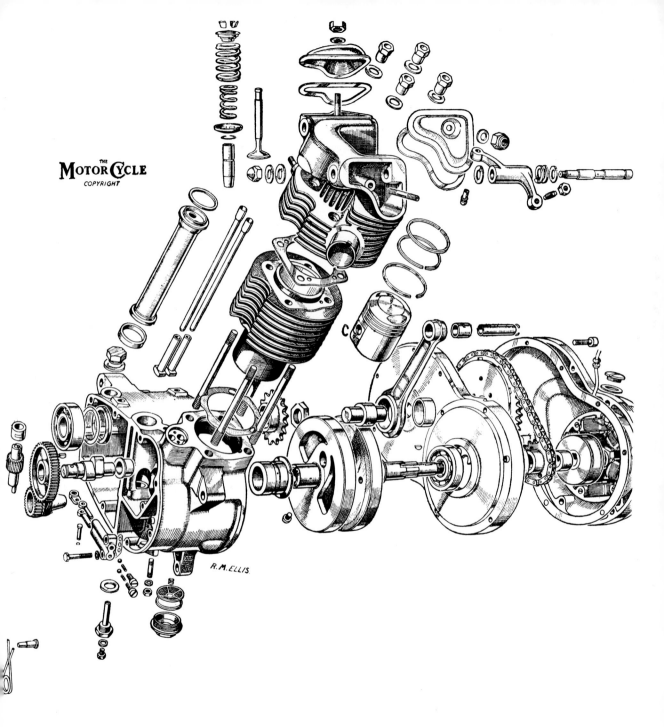

THE
MOTOR CYCLE
COPYRIGHT

R. M. ELLIS

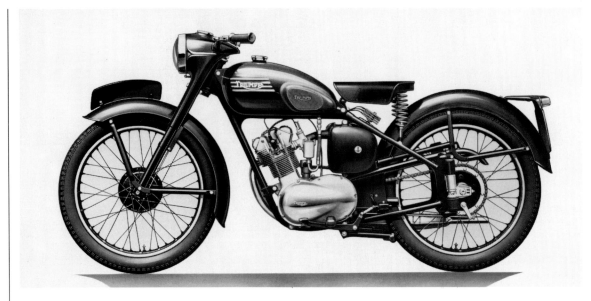

and extended back to include the gearbox to give unit construction and a light rigid structure. In the forward part it was open on the left to take the crankshaft with recesses on the right for the timing gear and oil pump. To the rear the arrangement was reversed with the casting open on the right to take the gearbox assembly and recessed on the left for the final drive sprocket.

The left side cover was spigoted into the crankcase and retained by a ring of screws. It carried the drive side main bearing, a ball race, and extended back to form the inner chaincase. The outer case was located by two dowels for in it was fitted the alternator stator. The rotor was keyed to the end of the crankshaft and the unit, along with the distrubutor and coil were new items introduced by Lucas for small machines with coil ignition. As was normal practice with a 6 volt system the output was controlled by the switching of the lights and in an emergency for starting with a flat battery the whole of the output could be directly coupled to the coil.

The primary transmission was by a single strand endless chain to a three plate clutch with the engine sprocket splined to the crankshaft and clamped in place by the rotor. The clutch contained a shock absorber and ran on a cast iron ring while the plates were driven by tags engaging with the drive sprocket. Three clutch springs were used and the pressure plate was lifted by a lever on the right and a pushrod running through the gearbox mainshaft.

The four-speed gearbox was very English in design and retained the usual features of mainshaft concentric with output sleeve gear, clutch and final drive both on the left and layshaft below mainshaft. Only the sleeve gear turned in a ball race, all the other bearings being bushes. One gear on each shaft was moved to select the ratios with the second on the mainshaft giving 3rd and top while the third on the layshaft gave 1st and 2nd.

The shafts were supported on the right by a cover that extended forward to enclose the timing gears and the oil pump in their compartments. In it were pressed the camshaft and gearbox bushes and it carried the clutch lever and its pivot.

Two selectors were used and these slid on a

Left **1954 Terrier with its family lines of nacelle and tank trim. Customers tended to stay with Triumph when they went bigger**

Right **In 1961 Anthony Smith bought this secondhand Cub and rode it from Cape Town to Cairo . . .**

Below **. . . and 20 years later he and his son used two Cubs to do the return journey**

cross-rod mounted ahead of the gearshafts. A quadrant selector plate was used pivoted on a pin mounted in the right cover and the plate carried slots for the positive stop mechanism as well as the two cam tracks. Its end was notched to provide gear detents for a leaf spring which was held in the crankcase by two screws.

The camplate pivot area was sealed off by a small cover held by two screws and ahead of it went the gear pedal shaft assembly. This pivoted in the crankcase and cover with twin spring loaded claw pins in a housing. Its rotating movement was restricted and a spring returned it to its mid-position. The pins were shaped to engage with the slots in the camplate and move it one gear at a time in response to movement of the external pedal.

To the rear of this mechanism went the kick-starter which engaged with bottom gear on the layshaft. Thus the machine had to be in neutral when being started but this arrangement did allow the rider to free the clutch first thing before each ride. The kickstart spring was outside the main cover and so was easy to change should it be necessary.

A further cover was fitted on the right to enclose the various items on that side and the two pedals were fitted outside that. The gear lever went on a spline so could be moved to suit the rider but the kickstart arm was retained by a cottar and thus was fixed in position.

A gear indicator was fitted and this device used a thin rod attached to the camplate near its pivot. The top end of the rod protruded through a hole in the top of the crankcase casting and was connected to a cable. This ran up to the nacelle to a rack and pinion mechanism which turned a hand round a dial to show which gear was engaged.

The main crankcase casting included three lugs for mounting the engine unit in the frame, one at each end and one on the underside. The frame was of the single loop type and equipped with plunger rear suspension. The main loop was a single tube bent to shape with its ends flattened into a D section. These two ends came together behind the headstock and formed a circular section which was brazed into the headstock, itself a malleable casting.

This method of construction placed heavy bending loads on the tubing at the join but gave a very low level top tube which meant that the petrol tank could dispense with the usual tunnel. The tank comprised just two pressings with the joint running along the sides on the line between the front and rear mountings which were to the headstock and the seat bracket so the tank contributed to frame strength. The tank itself was stiffened by a groove in the underside which also concealed the top tube, wiring and control cables.

The main frame loop had a malleable casting to carry the footrests and the same item was also used to support the lower chain stays. The upper stays were welded straight to the main loop and the stay ends joined by a fabricated assembly welded into place to carry the rear suspension. This plunger system used rods clamped into the ends of the frame on which slid light alloy wheel carriers with springs either side of them. Above went load springs under steel covers and below went the rebound springs inside gaiters. Drawbar chain adjusters bridged the fork ends.

At the front of the frame went telescopic forks which were damped only by the grease that lubricated them. Their construction was simple with internal springs but their appearance mirrored the big twins with fork covers and a headlamp nacelle. No steering damper was fitted and

Right above **The Anthony Smith Cub in 1983; note the hefty pannier frames**

Right **The plastic sheet used to shield the electrics on the 1956 Cub**

Far right **The rear subframe and pivoted fork introduced for the Cub in 1957**

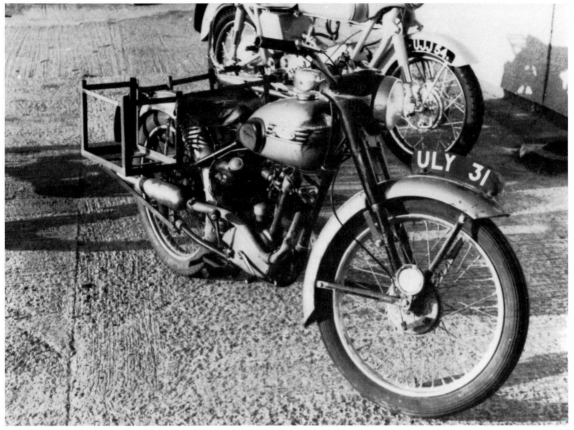

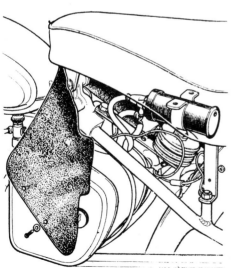

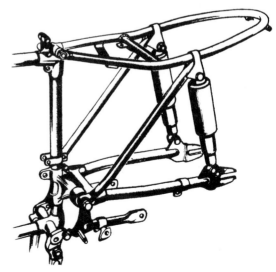

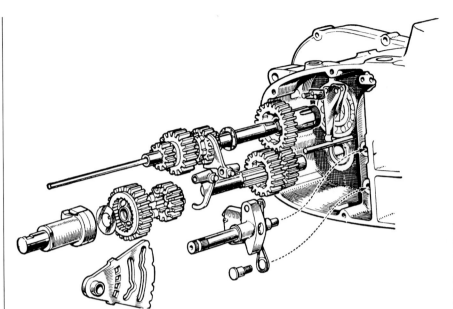

Left **Detail of the gearbox, gears and gearchange mechanism**

Right **The first model with the pivoted fork frame, the T20 as in 1958**

the fork ends were split with two bolts holding each end cap in place.

Both hubs were of the offset type in cast iron and fitted with single leading shoe drum brakes. The hub spindle was in one piece in both cases and the brake backplate a sliding fit on it at the rear but clamped up at the front. In both a single cam moved the shoes which pivoted on the same post. At the front that post was extended out to pick up with a lug behind the right fork leg to act as a brake anchor while at the rear the backplate was slotted to locate to a lug on the left wheel carrier of the plunger suspension. The rear brake was rod operated and the rear wheel drove the speedometer with the drive box on the right. The rear wheel sprocket was held by eight bolts with special small heads and in time a range of options was made available both for the rear wheel and the gearbox sprocket. Both rims carried studded pattern tyres of 2·75 × 19 in. size.

The mudguards fitted closely to the wheels and the front one was unsprung with a stay run-ning fore and aft on each side for support and a bridge to the fork legs. The rear one ran from the lower chain stays to a flare behind the wheel, below the neat number plate. The front plate, then a requirement, was a plain blade without the surround fitted to the twins.

The oil tank went on the right beneath the seat and blended into an air filter housing in the centre and toolbox plus battery housing on the left to make a single smooth unit. A rubber hose connected the filter to the carburettor and the petrol pipe ran neatly down to its left before turn-ing up to the base of the float chamber.

Rider comfort was looked after by a saddle fit-ted with barrel springs under which went the ignition coil. The footrest position was fixed and so was that of the bars in effect, as they were constrained by the nacelle. They were typically Triumph in style and extremely neat and unclut-tered with integral pivot blocks for clutch and brake levers and a built in horn button. No air lever was mounted on the bars as the cold start was assisted by a knob on the carburettor itself.

The nacelle thus carried the speedometer with the combined lights and ignition switch behind it. Inside went the horn and along each side a plated strip in the style of the bigger models. The tank carried kneegrips bearing the Triumph name and a badge trim of four bars carrying the company name, again in the same style as the larger models. A centre stand was provided for parking and the machine was finished in the traditional Triumph aramanth red with gold lining. The price was £98 basic which with the purchase tax payable in its home country made the total £125 4s 6d. Deliveries were forecast to begin in the spring of 1953. However, it was August, and thus the start of the 1954 season, before the first machines were sold.

In some ways the early models jumped the gun because once deliveries began so too did the problems which indicated that development testing had not been fully completed. Rather too many big ends failed and the clutch also proved troublesome with both plates and bearing. Otherwise the machine proved a success with

good performance, excellent fuel economy, good handling and brakes, and offering real style. A complete small motorcycle at a competitive price.

The early problems were quickly taken in hand and to demonstrate this to the dealers three machines ran from Lands End to John O'Groats under ACU supervision. To emphasize the point the riders were Edward Turner, Bob Fearon and Alec Masters who respectively designed, built and serviced the machine. All went well over the thousand miles which was routed past as many Triumph dealers as possible and the aims of 30 mph average and 100 mpg were easily exceeded. The figures came out at 36·68 mph and 108·61 mpg so the Terrier really proved its ability to commute.

In 1954 it was joined by a larger brother and itself received a number of detail improvements. Among them, the coil was moved to a position tucked in behind the gearbox and its place under the seat taken by the rectifier.

The Terrier continued in its amaranth red

Above **For off-road use, the late-1958 T20C with Zenith carburettor but incorrect tank badge**

Left **A T20C in use; the mudguards have been changed for some more suited to trials**

Right **Details of the Zenith 17MX carburettor**

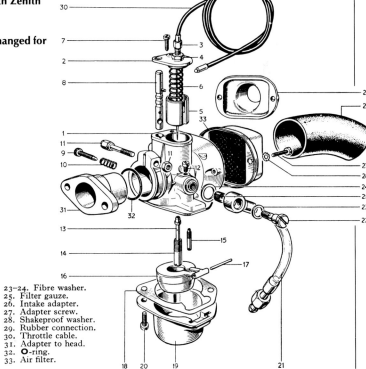

1. Carburetter body.
2. Mixing-chamber top.
3. Cable adjuster.
4. Adjuster lock-nut.
5. Throttle slide.
6. Slide spring.
7. Top-to-body screw.
8. Starter slide.
9. Throttle-stop screw.
10. Stop-screw spring.
11. Clamp nut and bolt.
12. Plug screw.
13. Emulsion tube.
14. Main jet.
15. Slow-running jet.
16. Float.
17. Float-hinge pin.
18. Joint washer.
19. Float bowl.
20. Float-bowl screw.
21. Petrol-feed pipe.
22. Union bolt.
23–24. Fibre washer.
25. Filter gauze.
26. Intake adapter.
27. Adapter screw.
28. Shakeproof washer.
29. Rubber connection.
30. Throttle cable.
31. Adapter to head.
32. O-ring.
33. Air filter.

finish with its saddle but could also be supplied fitted with a dual seat and pillion footrests. In the middle of the year it was changed internally by the adoption of a plain big end with the crankpin turning in a bush pressed into the connecting rod. This bush was in steel with a white metal bore.

Above **The T20 Cub in 1959 fitted with partial rear enclosure**

Right **1959 T20C with sports mudguards but still retaining nacelle**

The new, bigger, model was the Tiger Cub, destined to become far more popular than the Terrier and to outlive it by a dozen years. It was based very closely on the smaller machine but with the engine dimensions enlarged to 63×64 mm which gave a capacity of 199.5 cc. Compression ratio remained at 7.0:1, the cam timing was unaltered but the power was increased to 10 bhp at 6000 rpm.

The head, barrel and crankshaft were altered to suit the new dimensions and almost from the start the Cub had the plain big end. Its Amal carburettor was slightly larger than that of the Terrier and alternative exhaust systems were offered. The system from the smaller model could be had as an option, complete with its characteristic silencer but an upswept pipe was fitted as standard. This curled along the top line of the timing cover and below the oil tank to run straight back to the silencer.

The Cub had the gearing raised by one extra tooth on the gearbox sprocket and was fitted

with slightly fatter section tyres and a dualseat as standard. It also carried an 80 mph speedometer in place of the 70 mph one fitted to the Terrier and was finished in a pale shell blue sheen for the tank, mudguards and front brake backplate with the rest of the painted parts, including the hubs, in black. The rims were chrome plated with shell blue centres lined in black.

Further 1954 changes included a forged centre stand. The flywheel oilways were revised to provide a sludge trap which could be cleaned by removing a bolt in the wheel edge. Clutch action was improved by increasing the leverage at the gearbox end, fitting a heavy duty cable and adding an adjuster to the pressure plate.

For 1955 the upswept exhaust went so both models used the same system. On the electrical side life was made easier by adding snap connectors between the main switch and the wiring harness while a physically smaller and improved rectifier dealt with a higher charging rate. A prop stand became available as an option

but the finish remained unaltered.

The changes for 1956 were more deep rooted for the Cub than for the Terrier but on the smaller model there was an improved oil pump with increased output and a larger oil tank. The clutch friction material changed from inserted corks to bonded on segments and externally the bars were swept up more and a deeper rear chainguard fitted. The petrol tank design was modified to add a pair of internal struts to carry the loading between headstock and seat mounting without straining the tank joint. Legshields became an option for the Terrier.

The Cub was modified more extensively. It received all the Terrier changes and in its case the tank capacity was also increased to a round

three gallons while a good number of other changes were also included. Inside the engine went a stiffer big end crankpin, heavier flywheels and a half inch pitch primary chain. To accommodate this the chaincase was altered a little and the opportunity taken to move the filler plug into line with the clutch centre adjuster. The same case was also fitted to the Terrier.

The most noticeable change was to the wheel size which became 3·25 × 16 in. and in turn entailed other modifications. The frame was altered to ensure tyre clearance and the gearing raised to restore the ratio between engine and machine speeds. The new wheels used the same hubs as before and were shrouded by ribbed mudguards. The ignition coil was moved back

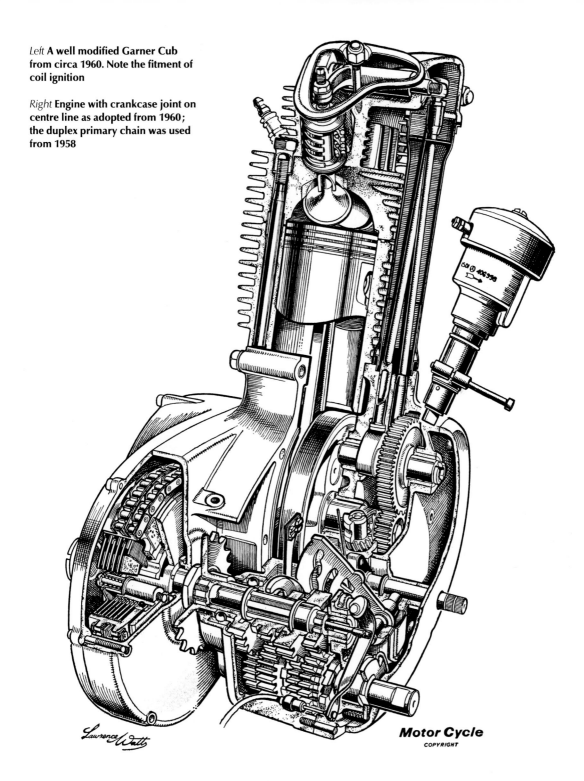

Left **A well modified Garner Cub from circa 1960. Note the fitment of coil ignition**

Right **Engine with crankcase joint on centre line as adopted from 1960; the duplex primary chain was used from 1958**

Lawrence Watts

Motor Cycle
COPYRIGHT

under the dualseat and both it and the rectifier were shielded by a plastic sheet attached to the seat mountings.

With the announcement of the changes late in 1955 came a road test of the Cub in *Motor Cycling*, the first to be carried out on a postwar single. In most respects the machine fulfilled its purpose with a recorded top speed of 67 mph and a fuel consumption around the 100 mpg mark most of the time. By wringing the engine's neck it reached 41 mph in second and 56 mph in third but at engine speeds of 7500 and 6700 rpm. In more usual riding the gears were good for 35 and 47 mph and the usual cruising speed was 55 mph.

Although the machine was small the riding position was good but the seat was a little short for two especially when wearing the bulky riding gear of the period. The suspension worked well enough and the fatter tyres dealt with the worst of the bumps. The brakes performed well and helped the machine maintain a respectable average on the road.

1956 saw the end of the Terrier but for some export markets a Cub with the Terrier engine continued to be available. For 1957 only the Cub was built, but in a new frame and two model forms. The first of these was the standard road T20 and the newcomer the T20C, a competition version with lights on the lines of later trail bikes. The new frame was used by both models and featured swinging fork rear suspension controlled by Girling units. At the front the frame

construction was unaltered but the loop was modified with lugs to take the seat tube behind the engine unit. This carried the support for the rear fork pivot while the rear sub-frame was bolted into place. Suitable lugs and brackets took the centre stand, prop stand, pillion rests and silencer mounting.

At the front the telescopic forks continued with the addition of simple hydraulic damping using a metering plug. The rear brake backplate was fitted with a torque stay which bolted to the fork leg and the wheel strength increased by fitting butted spokes to both flanges and not just on the sprocket side. The chainguard was made deeper and above the wheel the seat was restyled to suit the new frame and its sides extended to mask the coil and rectifier under it. The oil tank gained a froth tower to avoid oil loss via the tank breather but its capacity remained unchanged.

Inside the engine the big end and timing main bearing surface was changed to a heavier duty copper lead alloy coating and the crankpin spigot in the flywheels made larger. The primary chain tolerance was made tighter to avoid excess slack and the chaincase altered internally to give it a little more room. On the outside of the engine the rocker boxes gained some fins to help the heat dissipation.

The finish was changed to crystal grey and black in the same style as the earlier shell blue and the same colour was also used for the T20C. That model received all the changes of the road machine with one or two modifications to suit its purpose. Thus the frame rear cross-member was altered to give clearance to the tyre and the old type chainguard fitted. The fork legs were longer and the yokes strengthened. A fork bridge was added ahead of the legs. This helped to support the narrow front mudguard which was painted light alloy.

The model was based on that used by Ken Heanes to win a gold medal in the 1956 ISDT and although it retained lights and the nacelle,

Left above **The T20S of 1960, a model first sold in the USA in late 1958 and on to 1961**

Left **1962 T20SC for the USA. Heavy duty forks, direct lighting and Amal Monobloc.**

Above **An embryo street scrambler, the 1960 T20 S/A which was withdrawn**

Right above **Much as the earlier T20S, this is the 1961 T20 S/L built as a sports roadster. Also listed in scrambles form with upswept exhaust, off-road tyres and rev-counter option**

it was fitted out in off-road style to a degree. The upswept exhaust pipe of the first Cub was resurrected and a Trophy style silencer fitted to it. The gearing was lowered by going down one tooth on the gearbox sprocket and the tyres changed to Dunlop Trials Universals with a 3·00 × 19 in. on the front and a 3·50 × 18 in. at the rear. Butted spokes were fitted in the front wheel as well as the rear but the front mudguard continued to be close fitting and unsprung. A crankcase shield went under the engine and the prop stand was lengthened to cater for the larger wheels. No centre stand was fitted.

In April 1957 *The Motor Cycle* published a test of the Cub in its new frame and reached the same speeds as their rival. One of their early notes indicated that the air slide had been deleted from the carburettor without mention but despite this the machine started easily enough. They commented unfavourably on the engine noise as the valve gear clattered and the exhaust gave out a hard flat note of considerable volume on wide throttle openings. Certainly it

grated on the nerves and as such a model was bought mainly by young riders who used the throttle to keep up with the traffic the Cub soon had the reputation of being noisy.

The machine was light and easy to handle over all manner of roads and the brakes worked as well as ever. The new seat was better than its predecessor but remained on the hard side for long spells of riding. For commuting however, it was fine. The controls worked well and all fell to hand or foot easily except the dipswitch which sat out of reach on the right bar. A common problem of the times. Servicing continued to be easy and both stands worked well without effort.

Someone at Triumph must have listened to

the Cub and read the report as for 1958 it had a new and larger silencer. It also had a deeper section rear mudguard and some transmission changes it shared with the competition model. The primary chain became a duplex type and to accommodate this the outer case was made deeper. At the same time the clutch drum was changed to an iron casting with integral sprocket and internal slots to engage the friction plate tongues.

Due to the chain change the sprockets were again all revised to keep the overall ratio about the same but at the rear the size reduced from 54 to 46 teeth. The gearbox sprocket was also modified in form and the original felt seal behind it changed to a garter type. Conversion kits comprising the duplex chain, new sprockets and deep chaincase were offered to update earlier machines but this was not cheap so few were sold.

The frame of both models was modified in the headstock area with a lock socket. The lock itself was a separate item available as an option and

the machine was secured by inserting the lock body into the socket and then turning and removing the key. On the T20C only, plastic gaiters were added to the front forks to exclude dirt.

In the middle of the 1958 season the carburettor was changed to a 17 mm Zenith with integral air filter for the road model although the competition one retained its air box by the oil tank.

1959 brought further engine changes with increased finning for the barrel. In plan they were in pear shape and tapered to the front while the new casting also had a more robust base flange and its stud holes cast into the iron so the studs themselves could no longer be seen between the fins. A double seal, back to back, went behind the gearbox sprocket in place of the single seal adopted the year before with one keeping the oil in and the other the dirt out. The area around the sprocket was enlarged to allow the fitment of one with more teeth.

On the T20 road model alone the rear of the machine was partly enclosed by the addition of

Above **1961 T20 for the USA, hence special bars**   *Below* **The home market 1961 T20**

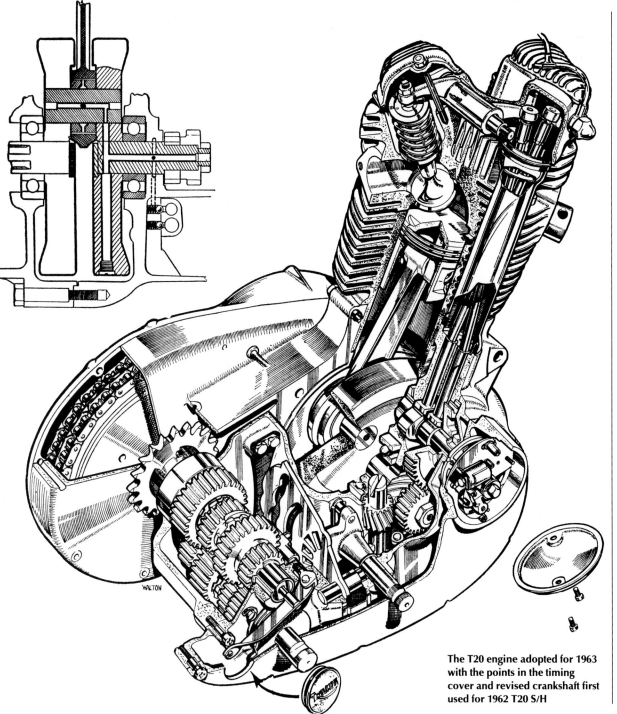

WALTON

The T20 engine adopted for 1963
with the points in the timing
cover and revised crankshaft first
used for 1962 T20 S/H

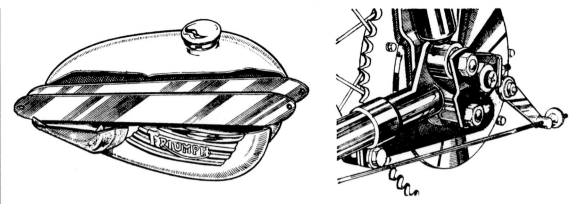

Above **To left the tank bracing strut and right the outrigger support for the suspension unit stud of the TR20 and TS20 The support was used by all sports Cubs but never the T20**

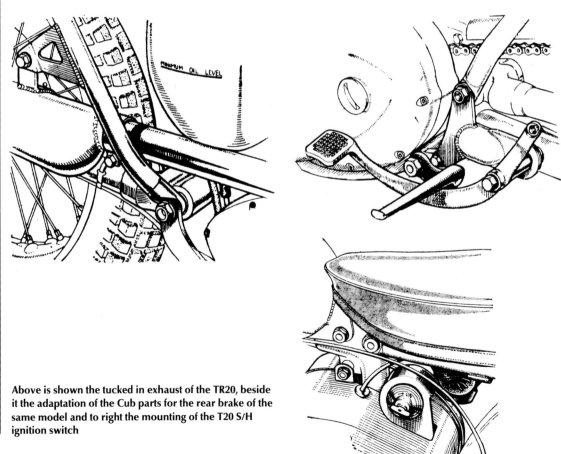

Above is shown the tucked in exhaust of the TR20, beside it the adaptation of the Cub parts for the rear brake of the same model and to right the mounting of the T20 S/H ignition switch

The 1962 T20S/H which was based on the T20S/L and continued as a sports road machine

two side panels. These ran from beneath the seat aft of the rear unit fixings down to the gearbox and forward round the seat tube. The oil tank and toolbox were moved back and allowed to project through the side panels to remain accessible and to avoid a colour clash the two items were finished in the same crystal grey as the panels. The oil tank cap was moved to the top forward corner of the tank while a new petrol tank was also fitted. This was deeper, although the capacity remained three gallons, and had new style badges in the form adopted by the twins a year or two earlier.

As the new decade approached the Cub began to undergo a series of changes and over the next few years new versions and different colour schemes were used to try to maintain sales. It was to be a time when the market shrunk and then changed but through much of it the Cub ran on fulfilling its basic role as a means of transport.

For 1960, the T20S, first seen in the USA late in 1958, came into the UK list to replace the T20C. The engine in both the newcomer and the road machine received a larger inlet valve and a modified cylinder head with the exhaust port moved round to give more clearance between the pipe and the frame down tube. The carburettor size increased to 18 mm and although it remained a Zenith it gained a float tickler and a choke. At the other end of the system went a silencer with a mute in the tailpipe. This took the form of a long fluted cone which was claimed to reduce the end noise of the exhaust. External changes on the T20 were the fitting of 17 in. wheels, still with 3·25 in. section tyres, and a smaller gearbox sprocket to lower the gearing to match. The amount of oil in the chaincase was also reduced.

The new model, the T20S, was cast much in the mould of its predecessor but benefited from a new set of front forks. These were based on the ones fitted to the 350 cc twin, were gaitered and carried a small headlamp shell on ears welded to the top covers. The forward front mudguard stays were shortened and ran to a higher point on the fork leg. The engine was as used by the road model complete with its changes for 1960 but the overall gearing was lower than that used by the T20C. In addition close or wide ratio sets of internal gears were fitted in the case, as needed.

The electric system was very different with energy transfer ignition and direct lighting, each powered by a pair of alternator coils. In theory the energy transfer system was fine with the power from the coils being fed to the ignition system in a sharp pulse when the points opened to induce the secondary voltage to create the spark. In practice it was essential that the points opened at a time when the alternating current output was at a peak and as this had a sharp

Above **1963 T20 S/H with gear position plunger in crankcase top, timing case points and finned rocker box covers**

Right **The 1963 TR20 trials model, no lights and well tucked in**

point timing was critical.

On the Cub the rotor was keyed to the crankshaft and so was positioned accurately to the ignition point by normal working tolerances. Likewise, the stator was held to the chaincase but between them there could be a variation, from machine to machine of the exact point of peak output. The timing side was much worse for between the crankshaft and the points lay two gear pairs, one a skew notorious for its backlash, an advance mechanism and a cam bearing.

Needless to say the relation between all the parts varied and it was quickly found that points gap and timing were very critical. The machine soon had a reputation for either starting but not running or running but not starting.

The lighting side was very simple and no battery was fitted. The feed from the alternator went to a push switch in the headlamp shell which turned the head and tail lights on. A second matching switch gave main or dip beam and a separate line connected the electric horn to a push button on the left bar. For trials use the headlamp could easily be removed thanks to a connector under the tank.

The tyre sizes remained as before but the rear fork was modified to allow a 4 in. section cover to be fitted. A small D shaped speedometer was mounted above the headlamp on the top fork crown.

Not many of the 1960 models were built before there was a further radical engine change which although major left all the internals as they were. Starting with export T20S models the change was soon incorporated in all Cubs and moved the crankcase split line over to the centre of the cylinder. It thus followed convention in this feature and two new crankcase castings were required to do this. They were much on the lines of the earlier ones and the right side continued to include the complete gearbox shell which extended out to the left past the joint face.

Nearly everything else stayed the same although the distributor clamp was simplified to a single screw. This was also a timing cover fixing so when the cover was removed care was needed to avoid disturbing the ignition setting. The cylinder studs were shortened a little, just enough to allow the head to come off without having to lower the engine in the frame.

During 1961 the T20S was replaced by two models, one aimed more directly at trials and the other at scrambles, or rather at enduros, for it retained its lights. The road model continued and all were fitted with a new oil pump with greatly increased output, a part of which was bled off to lubricate the skew gears driving it and the distributor. Energy transfer ignition was retained for the competition models typed T20T and T20S/L along with the lighting coils plus an additional one to allow a stop light to be added if desired. The same models also had a toolbox fitted under

53

the seat while the scrambler had a rev-counter option available. When supplied with this the standard D speedometer was replaced by a small round magnetic one to pair with the rev-counter head.

All three power units used the same basic engine but while the T20 and T20T retained the features of earlier units the scrambler was tuned. Thus it had a piston giving a compression ratio of 9·0:1, a sports camshaft and an Amal Monobloc carburettor which combined to push the power up to 14·5 bhp at 6500 rpm. All three gearboxes were fitted with different sets of ratios with the wide going into the T20T, a close set going into the T20S/L and T20S, and the T20 retaining its usual standard gear set.

All the models were given a new finish which included two colours for the petrol tank with the road model in black and silver, and the competition ones in ruby red and silver. The latter also retained their old style four bar badges on the smaller size petrol tank.

Motor Cycling road tested a T20 in February 1961 and a T20S/L two months later. The first continued to offer its mid-sixties top speed and 100 mpg plus economy just as in the past, if anything it consumed even less petrol thanks to the Zenith carburettor. This was fitted with a cold start knob which helped to bring the engine to life on cold mornings. In other respects the machine performed well and quietly thanks to its improved and muted silencer while handling and brakes were up to standard. The tool kit was thought to be meagre with a couple of omissions despite which it proved awkward to pack in the small space provided. Otherwise maintenance was easy to carry out.

Top left **The T20 in 1964 with gear indicator**

Left **And in 1965, no indicator which can hardly have worried Soichiro Honda**

Much of this also applied to the faster T20S/L which clocked speeds close to the legal 70 limit with rider seated normally and 78 mph when flat on the tank. Consumption fell to around 90 mpg and the energy transfer ignition called for a very determined prod on the kickstarter, often preceded by pulling the engine back on compression. The exhaust was a touch noisier than on the standard model despite the mute but the tighter valve clearances of the sports camshaft reduced engine rattle.

The handling was fine with the front forks and their two way damping keeping the wheel glued to the ground although both suspensions were a little on the hard side. The brakes continued to work well except that the front juddered when used at top speed and the simple lighting system proved adequate for night riding.

In October 1961 the models for the next year were announced with the T20T being dropped and the T20S/L becoming the T20S/S. This was to be a very interim move for a further and more major change came early in 1962.

As far as the October news was concerned the T20 was fitted with an Amal carburettor for some export markets but remained faithful to the Zenith at home. The new T20S/S was really just the 1961 model with a new type number but for the trials enthusiasts could be fitted with the low compression engine as an option while the high level exhaust pipe could be picked out from the existing spares list.

Both models in the range were fitted with an improved oil pump with cast iron body, a new petrol tap and a larger taillight with integral reflector so the separate one was no longer needed. The sports model was given a new colour for its tank top in polychromatic burgundy while retaining the silver and black for the other parts.

Three new models were listed from February 1962, one a replacement for the T20S/S which did, however, continue to be sold up to 1965. All used a revised engine with a ball race timing main bear-

START RIGHT-WITH TRIU

Every Triumph machine which leaves the modern factory at Meriden has behind it the unsurpassed wealth of more than sixty years' experience. The 1965 range comprises ten models, each of which has been designed and developed to suit the individual requirements of discerning riders. Whatever you seek in a motorcycle, whether it be for everyday economical travel, healthy sport, pleasure or the sheer satisfaction of supreme performance, there is a Triumph model designed to suit you perfectly. Specifications are comprehensive, but one factor is constant and that is the supreme standard of quality guaranteed by the insignia on every new Triumph machine "Holder of the World Motorcycle Speed Record". This constancy is further underlined by the long history of successes in the International Six Days' Trial culminating in the Triumph Team of 350 c.c. and 650 c.c. machines winning a Manufacturers team award in the 1964 event — and in addition six Gold Medals.

200 c.c. Lightweight range

The 200 c.c. range appeals strongly to those who want their first machine to look and perform like a larger model, but essentially need a really safe, sensible, economical method of personal transport.

350 c.c. and
500 c.c. Medium-weight range

For the rider who combines everyday transport with substantial mileage for pleasure and objective journeys, the 350 c.c. and 500 c.c. twins are the perfect choice for all conditions.

650 c.c. Twin cylinder range

Power and tractability are blended in the three 650 c.c. twins so successfully that these models have no equal on the road for perfection of performance. Unobtrusive in the town, unsurpassable on the highway, these are machines designed to provide the most experienced rider with the last word in satisfaction.

SPORTS CUB

200 c.c.

REAR CHAIN GUARD ON SPORTS CUB IS EXTENDED TO GIVE IMPROVED CHAIN PROTECTION.

For the truly sporting lightweight enthusiast this model offers crisp four-stroke acceleration and economy with first-class handling and suspension. In full road-going trim and readily adaptable to most forms of competition, this sparkling lightweight has immediate appeal to the younger rider.

Not illustrated
TR20 Trials Cub
Special competition model built to the identical specification of the models used by Triumph works riders. Full details on request.

Page from the 1965 catalogue showing the T20 S/H which had a cranked kickstart that year

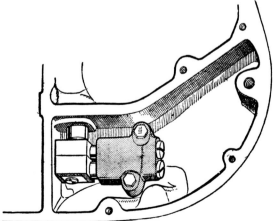

Above **The 1965 T20 S/H which also had new fork sliders**

Left **Revised oil pump drive adopted for the 1966 range**

ing and stiffer big end with altered oilways. The new crankpin was of two part construction with a hardened bearing ring pressed onto a plain shaft. The working diameter was increased with the bearing surface still on the inside of the liner pressed into the big end eye of the connecting rod.

The timing side was modified with a shaft pressed into the flywheel to replace the integral stub. This shaft was extended out through both skew and timing gears, which were made as separate items, and these retained by an end nut.

Oil pump capacity was raised and fed into the hollow timing shaft via drillings in the crankcase casting to a point just outboard of the main bearing. The case was machined to give a small running clearance to the mainshaft and the oil thus encouraged into the shaft from where it was passed via more drillways to the bearing surface. The sludge trap was kept.

The new road model was typed the T20S/H and continued the theme of earlier models as a sports machine although the off-road aspect was much reduced with a ribbed front tyre. The electrics were changed to drop the troublesome energy transfer and reverted to plain coil ignition with emergency start. The wiring was kept simple by mounting both ignition and light switches under the seat close to the battery, rectifier and coil with one switch on each side. The dip switch stayed in the headlamp shell, now in the centre, and the D speedometer remained. A connector allowed the shell to be easily removed for competition if this was desired.

Of the other two models the TR20 was for trials and the TS20 for scrambles. Both had many common features which included the new crankshaft, main bearing and the old energy transfer ignition. They also shared a short seat and a frame with a bend in the right seat stay that allowed the exhaust to run inside it. The scrambler used a high level open pipe which ran back to the rear wheel spindle while the trials model was fitted with a barrel shaped silencer taken from the TR6 Trophy 650 cc model.

The trials model was fitted with a one piece chainguard that contrived to protect both chain runs and the machine footrests and rear brake pedal were moved rearwards a little just as on the works models. On both competition machines the rests were braced with stays and the pivot bolt that joined the suspension leg to the rear fork was strengthened by an added outer plate. Both machines sported polished alloy mudguards and the heavy duty fork with gaiters. Differences amounted to compression ratios and wide or close gearboxes, the top gear ratio being the same for both.

The Cubs continued to be popular and all four ran on into 1963 with some noticeable changes to the engine. First, and of great help to the energy transfer ignition, was the move of the points into the timing cover. There, the cam was driven via its advance mechanism straight off the end of the camshaft thus removing much of the backlash in the drive. A chrome plated cover gave easy access to the points.

The new timing cover had a hole added aft of the kickstart pedal shaft, which was usually blanked off with a rubber bung. Removal of this gave access to the end of the clutch cable so it could be changed without having to take the cover off. A further change was at the top of the engine where finned rocker covers were adopted, still with the single bolt fixing.

On the road models the gearbox position dial went and was replaced by a plunger which rose out of the gearbox casting to show which ratio was in mesh. An oil tank drain plug was added which helped mainly on the enclosed T20, and the rectifier became the Lucas miniature silicon type.

The T20 was modified internally to bring it into line with the other models with the newer crankshaft and ball bearing timing side main. Its electrics were also modified to twin switches in the nacelle, one each for ignition and lights. The sporting T20S/H was given the option of a rev-counter and the drive for this was taken from the old distributor housing and the oil pump shaft. The colours of all models remained as they were except that the oil tank and toolbox lid on the T20 were painted to match the tank top and contrast with the enclosure panels.

A further *Motor Cycle* road test early in the year showed the sports Cub to be as quick as ever, still with rather firm suspension and still doing an acceptable job. No choke was fitted so the carburettor had to be flooded before a cold start and the short kickstart lever meant a firm prod was needed to push the engine over its 9:1 ratio. Brakes and handling were as always and the tucked in bars and footrests were an aid in town or country riding.

The models, less the TS20, ran into 1964 with minor changes only to the mechanics but a new finish in hi-fi scarlet and silver for all. In the engine went a one-piece crankpin of the same dimensions as used from 1962, an oil pump skew drive gear in aluminium bronze to increase wear resistance and reshaped shock absorber rubbers in the clutch centre.

The two road machines had a combined horn button and dipswitch fitted while the sports one had the rear chainguard extended down to give protection to the lower chain run.

A survey carried out by the *Motor Cycle* in 1964 indicated why the Cub was so popular with most owners very pleased with their machines and the support given them by factory and dealer. In most areas the small Triumph scored high marks and did its job well. It seemed that reliability was rather dependant on the owner with some engines running well for long periods and others suffering problems with mains and big end. The fact that many machines were owned by learners indicated both a reason and a shortcoming in the design for such treatment should have been expected and foreseen.

Other complaints concerned the poor horn, rather average lights, inadequate toolkit, awkward panels on the standard model and rather rattly engine. The paint and chrome were good and new machines reached customers in good order.

Later in the year *Motor Cycling* ran a review type article and road test which showed that in terms of performance the Cubs had changed little over the years. Improvements were aimed at increasing the engine's endurance and changes were otherwise detail developments from year to year. It was only on looking back to the first Cub that their sum total became apparent. By that time, in the middle of 1964, some 100,000 small singles had been produced.

The range of Cubs for 1965 had limited alterations. The gear indicator on the road models went and the sports model was fitted with a longer kickstart pedal which was cranked to clear the silencer and still folded out of the way when not in use. Front fork leg construction was changed with the spindle lug formed integrally with the slider instead of being brazed in place.

An offshoot was the export only T20SM Mountain Cub sold to the USA for use as a trail bike. To ensure safety for owners in the hills it was painted bright yellow to put hunters off. Other Cubs finished up wearing khaki and on duty with armed forces in Europe. They were equipped with panniers and other service items, and listed as the T20WD and T20MWD.

The 1966 range showed the first sign of the parent company hand reaching out from the BSA plant at Small Heath. It was a time when the whole group began to run into trouble and it was in the mid-1960s that the seeds were sown. Edward Turner had retired in 1964 and after him came men from outside the industry with no experience of motorcycles.

As the years went by the product became a consumer durable, a group research centre was set up and innumerable unneeded executives appeared on the group organization chart. Many of the older men with deep experience of motorcycles and the industry either left or were swept into minor positions in the corner.

The effect on the Cub was an amalgamation with the BSA Bantam. The front fork legs of the two machines had been virtually common for some time and for 1966 the basic frame was also adopted. The engine mountings were modified to suit the three lugs on the Cub, the Bantam had two pairs of bolts fore and aft, and the rear frame was standard Bantam.

The hubs were already common as the BSA had used the cast iron Cub items for some years so they already fitted both front and rear fork ends. The headlamp shell was Bantam, long enough to carry the speedometer and switches, and finished by chrome plating. In the centre of the machine the BSA form panels were used and a new oil tank made to match them. A Bantam tank was fitted carrying the T20 type badge and a dualseat with centre handgrip was used. The mudguards were Bantam and the wheel size 18 in. front and rear.

Inside the engine of the new version of the Cub and those of the T20S/H and T20SM, both of which continued, went a new oil pump drive. This retained the pump in its existing position and also the vertical drive shaft. The lower end of this was machined as an offset pin and this

connected to the pump plungers with a sliding block as used by other Triumphs for many years. The big end was also changed and after years of modifications to the plain type it became a roller bearing and trouble free.

On the outside the appearance changed with the adoption of head and barrel castings with more of a square cross-section. They continued in alloy and iron respectively, the latter still finished in an aluminium colour, and the engines became known as the square barrel type.

A road test of the Cub in its new Bantam frame showed it still to be good for the middle 60s in speed and an easy 100 mpg. The two halves married together well and the result was a slightly bigger machine but one that was quite acceptable. As with older Cubs and Bantams, the road-holding, steering and brakes were fine while the valve gear continued to rattle.

The Cub range offered a good start to the new rider but group policy was to concentrate on the big twins. To this end the Cub production was switched to Small Heath and few of the true Meriden models survived 1966. The trials machine lapsed early in the year and the much loved sports model went during the summer. This left the standard T20, albeit in its BSA frame,

The Bantam Cub T20 of 1966 using the BSA frame, forks and other cycle parts

Super Value from the very centre of England—

.....the new

TRIUMPH

SUPER CUB 200

Here's a sparkling new addition to the Triumph range—the Super Cub 200—an attractive new version of the popular Tiger Cub.

It's nippy, easy to handle, economical to run, and in its new Flamboyant Bushfire Red, even more appealing in appearance than its predecessor.

Modern style petrol tank, chromium-plated headlamp, full-width hubs, new type dual seat with safety strap—these are new features which make the Super Cub super value.

End of the line, the 1967 T20 S/C Super Cub with Bantam tank, full width hubs and other minor changes. Ran into 1968, then stopped

and this was announced as continuing unchanged for 1967. In fact it was dropped at the end of the year and replaced by a revised model.

This was the T20 Super Club which was much on the same lines. Engine, frame and forks were unaltered as was the centre panelling and many of the details. New items were the hubs which became full width front and rear although they retained the same brake working diameter. A good silencer that really muted the exhaust was fitted and a revised front mudguard mounting was used. This was in the style fitted to many of the earlier sports Cubs with the forward stays

running to a point halfway up the fork leg. From the same point a second stay ran up and over the mudguard to act as a fork bridge.

A new finish in Bushfire red was adopted and the petrol tank was a Bantam type with a chrome plated area on each side. New badges were used but in an old style with four bars and the Triumph name much as in the past.

The Cub was nearing the end of its days for it had no place in the future plans of the group management. It continued into 1968 without change but the next year went from the range. Mourned by owners and dealers alike it effectively removed Triumph from the learner and commuter market place for their 250 cc single and baby scooter offerings failed to fill the gap.

So, after a decade and a half, the Cub was no more and joined the Terrier as a memory.

3 | Tigress and Tina

Triumph Tigress scooter with the 175 cc single engine, not often seen

In the postwar years while Triumph concentrated on their twins, BSA, who owned them, dipped a toe into the scooter market once or twice during the 1950s. None of these attempts were either successful or sustained, but in the end the group had to accept that scooters were not going to go away and that at that time they represented a sizeable chunk of the market.

The result was an announcement made in 1957 that a prototype scooter, designed by Edward Turner, had been undergoing tests. The press statement went on to say that the machine would be offered in both the Triumph and Sunbeam ranges by mid-1958 and would have a good performance allied to the usual scooter weather protection.

It was October 1958 before the formal press presentation was made, although the existence of the new machines had been an open secret for many months. Two versions of the scooter were shown, each available as a Triumph Tigress or a BSA Sunbeam, one fitted with a 175 cc two-stroke engine based on the BSA Bantam dimensions and the other powered by a 250 cc twin cylinder four-stroke.

Behind the crankcase the two engine and gearbox units were the same and the only differences in the cycle parts of the two marques were the badges and colours.

The two-stroke version had engine dimensions of 61·5 × 58 mm for its single cylinder making the capacity 172 cc. Construction of the top

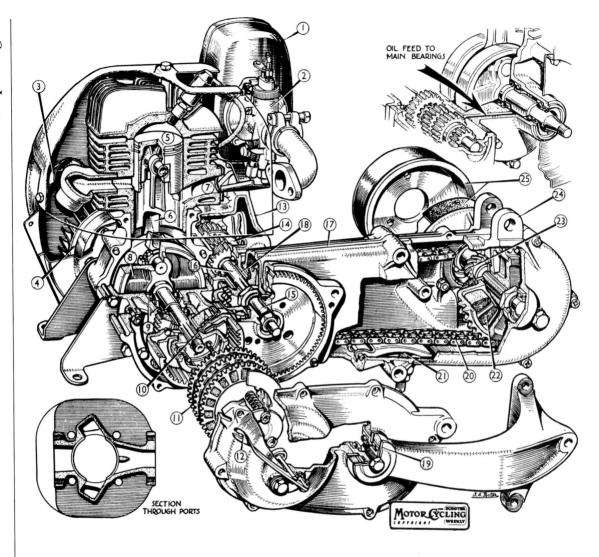

OIL FEED TO
MAIN BEARINGS

SECTION
THROUGH PORTS

MOTOR CYCLING
COPYRIGHT
SCOOTER
WEEKLY

Engine and
transmission of
the single, a
combination
of Bantam
technology, Cub
gearbox and the
rest common to
the twin scooter

━━━━━━━━ **K E Y** ━━━━━━━━

1: Air cleaner
2: Amal carburetter
3: Cowling with air deflector to exhaust
   port
4: Cooling fan and generator
5: Piston with cutaway skirt to clear
   transfer port
6: Transfer port
7: Forked inlet port
8: Flywheel assembly with pressed in
   mainshafts and crankpin
9: Main bearings sealed from crankcase
   and independently lubricated
10: Primary drive gears
11: Six plate clutch on engine shaft
12: Clutch operating arm

13: Four speed gearbox cast integral with
   crankcase
14: Gear selector complete with fork
15: Gearbox input shaft
16: Gearbox outboard shaft
17: Rear chaincase also acting as swinging
   arm
18: Swinging arm inner bearing
19: Swinging arm outer bearing
20: Duplex chain final drive
21: Chain adjuster
22: Shock absorber in rear sprocket
23: Speedometer drive
24: Rear suspension unit attachment lug
25: Rear brake

ANNOUNCING THE

SLEEKEST SMOOTHEST SCOOTER EVER

MODEL TS 1. 172-c.c.
Two-stroke, 4 speeds.
Price £164 19s. 8d.
(Incl. £32 14s. 8d. P.T.).

MODEL TW 2. 249-c.c.
O.H.V. Twin, 4 speeds.
Price £187 2s. 6d.
(Incl. £37 2s. 6d. P.T.).

MODEL TW 2s. As TW 2
but with electric self-starter.
Price £200 17s. 0d.
(Incl £39 17s. 6d. P.T.).

This is the "Tigress"—a magnificent new scooter by TRIUMPH. Choose your engine—simple two-stroke or lively o.h.v. twin, both with 4-speed gearbox. Controls?—Simpler than any car. Styling?—Look at the beautiful lines. Comfort?—Hydraulically controlled supension front and rear, and a supple full-length Latex-filled seat. Safety?—Powerful 5-inch brakes and hairline steering. Interested?—Send for the **TRIUMPH TIGRESS folder, fully illustrated in colour.**

TRIUMPH Tigress

TRIUMPH ENGINEERING CO. LTD., SCOOTER DIVISION, Dept. No. 13, WAVERLEY WORKS, BIRMINGHAM, 10

1958 advert for the Tigress listing all three models, duplicated under the BSA label

half and crankshaft followed the same lines as the Bantam but only a few items were the same: the port timing was, for example, but the actual barrel, still cast in iron, differed in respect of the exhaust stub. The head was Bantam in light alloy with the plug laid back to the rear and both it and the barrel went onto four long studs screwed into the crankcase. Nuts secured them, the rear pair long sleeve ones that supported the cooling cowl around the upper engine.

The piston with its two rings was Bantam as was the connecting rod and big end, an uncaged roller assembly running directly on crankpin and in the rod eye. The flywheels copied the BSA style but although of the same width they were much smaller in diameter. The mainshafts were both longer to suit the installation and pressed into the flywheels.

Each was supported by a pair of ball races with one oil seal inboard of them and working on a machined diameter of the flywheel and the other outboard. This isolated the four main bearings from the engine mixture and they were lubricated, as on the Bantam, by a bleed feed from the gearbox.

The crankcase was split on its vertical centre line with the gearbox contained entirely in the right part. The right mainshaft extended out of the case and carried a Wico-Pacy generator with both lighting and ignition coils. The points and ignition condensor were mounted on the stator with access via apertures in the rotor which embodied cooling fan vanes.

On the left end of the crankshaft went a three plate clutch with three pressure springs. The design was the reverse of normal motorcycle practice so that the clutch release lever went on the left of the engine unit and pushed into the clutch body to free the plates. The clutch drove from its centre on the mainshaft to the drum and this had a gear fixed to its back between it and the outer main bearing. This gear meshed with one mounted behind it on an extended gearbox mainshaft.

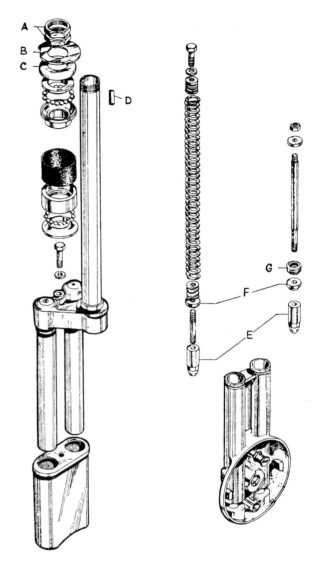

One-sided front fork used by the scooter with twin tubes and single leg. One housed the spring and the other the damper

The gearbox was traditional English with four speeds and both it and the positive stop mechanism and the selectors were based on the Cub. Thus the sleeve gear carrying the final drive sprocket was concentric with the mainshaft and below it in bushes ran the layshaft. The two selectors were positioned on a cross-rod behind the gears and the quadrant selector plate went behind that. It pivoted on a pin mounted horizontally in the gearbox end cover.

Unlike the Cub the plate was extended out to the opposite side of its pivot and this area contained the positive stop slots while the outer edge was notched for the location of a spring loaded pin. A positive stop assembly with two spring loaded plungers moved the camplate and was linked with a rod to a forward mounted pedal. A second pedal, well to the rear and moved by the rider's right heel, selected neutral from the second gear position.

A third pedal on the right was the kickstarter which unlike a motorcycle was expected to work in a forward direction. To enable this to happen and to rotate the gearbox layshaft in the correct direction a chain was used to link the two items each of which was fitted with a small sprocket. Inside the box the starter pawl worked on the layshaft gear as in the Cub. An outer cover enclosed the gearchange mechanism and helped to support the pedal shafts.

The final drive was by a duplex chain running in a beam which acted as both chaincase and swinging arm for the rear suspension. This arm pivoted on the gearbox mainshaft centre and was built up from a pair of mating light alloy castings plus a further out-rigger casting. The first two pivoted on a bearing set behind the gearbox sprocket and outboard of them the primary drive case and its cover extended back. The outrigger went outside of these items with its own bearing and picked up on three studs in the main chaincase inside of which went a chain slipper tensioner with an adjuster bolt set underneath in the case.

The engine and transmission unit was carried in a frame with bolted on headstock. The main

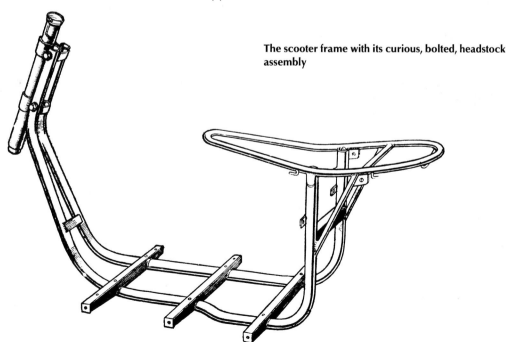

The scooter frame with its curious, bolted, headstock assembly

67

Above **Tigress cheesecake photo, the attached release quotes a production target of 50,000 a year**

Left **Well laden Tigress with a number of the accessories offered for it**

frame comprized two tubes which ran parallel at the steering head before diverging as they ran down and back. After running under the engine and gearbox they turned up again and were joined at the top by a tube shaped to match the base of the dualseat. This tube was braced to the main frame which had three major cross beams to join the two tubes and support the bodywork.

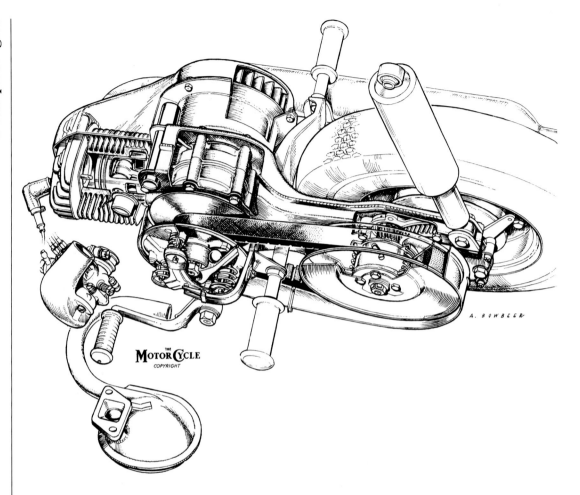

The Tina engine with vee belt automatic transmission, hub gear reduction and engine safety switch

At the front the fork headstock tube carried two clips which went between the main frame tubes with cross bolts to hold the assembly together. The forks were one sided with the twin tubes fixed to the bottom crown secured in turn to the headstem. Both tubes were on the left of the machine to enable stub axle mounted wheels to be fitted.

The lower moving part of the fork was a single alloy casting with two holes bored in it to correspond with and slide onto the twin tubes under a pressed shroud. One tube and hole concealed the suspension spring and the other contained

the hydraulic damper. At the top of the fork stem went adjuster nuts and above them the handlebar was clamped into place with an in-built steering lock. The rear suspension was controlled by a single spring and damper unit on the left.

Both wheels were pressed steel and of 10 in. diameter shod with 3·50 in. tyres. They were interchangeable and fitted onto three studs in the brake drum with a hub cap to conceal the nuts. Both brakes were drum with a single leading shoe and their operation was by right hand for the front and left foot for the rear. The clutch and throttle followed motorcycle practice and the handlebar controls were completed by a group on the left for dipswitch, horn and ignition cut-out. A further switch on the left of the speedometer controlled the lights.

The bodywork of the scooter was built up from steel pressings bolted together to form the front mudguard, apron, instrument panel, footboard and engine cover. The handlebars also had a small pressed cover, the battery was carried on the left of the apron in a compartment under a lid. Under the hinged seat went the toolkit with each item recessed into a moulded rubber tray and at the rear was the fuel tank, its filler concealed by the seat. Unlike the 250 which had its silencer in the tail of the body, the 175 bore this under the engine in front of the rear wheel, with a small tailpipe exiting to the right.

The machine was listed at £164 19s 8d and offered with a range of accessories including a windscreen, spare wheel and carrier. The usual shopping bag hook was fitted to the rear of the apron as standard.

The model was launched at Grosvenor House in London with celebrities Harry Secombe and Stirling Moss among those present; the upper house was represented by Lord Brabazon. Some prophecies as to future sales were made, but in time these proved to be optimistic as the venture was none too successful in either engine form.

It was April 1960 before *Motor Cycling* road tested a 175 cc Tigress and early in their report they noted that the owner was encouraged to do little more than very elementary servicing. This came about because access was limited to two small panels unless the major pressings were dismantled and this contrasted strongly with the popular Lambretta with its detachable sides.

The machine cruised happily at 45–50 mph and was good for 55 mph with windscreen fitted. It returned over 90 miles to each gallon of petrol

in flat country but more was used if the terrain was hilly or a passenger was carried. The steering was fine above 12 mph but lacked castor action below this speed while the brakes worked well from any speed. The seat and riding position were comfortable for a reasonable length of time.

Some aspects of the Tigress such as the fuel tap and cold starting were rather motorcycle orientated compared with Italian scooters. In the traditions of Triumph the clutch tended to stick so the first gear engagement of the day was abrupt. No mention of the ease or otherwise of using the centre stand was made in the test or in one of a 250 cc Tigress in *The Motor Cycle*.

The Tigress, along with the other group scooters, continued with little change other than colour over the years. The quoted compression ratio went up and down from the original figure of 7·5:1. From very early on this was reduced to 6·5 and then in the middle of 1960 it rose again to 7·6. In truth there was some doubt as references other than factory material quote 6·8 and 7·4 or a general figure of 7:1. The higher ratio did call for more ignition advance and all the figures were geometric ratios and so low compared with those from later years.

In 1961 the gearing was lowered by changing the number of teeth on both final drive and rear wheel sprockets. By going down at the front and up one at the rear the chain pitches remained at 94 and the small variation was within the capability of the tensioner.

That year colour options in a two tone finish were made available but otherwise the model ran on unaltered until the middle of 1965 when it was dropped.

Before then however, in 1962, it was joined by another scooter, this one smaller and aimed at the mass market. The idea of a simple, cheap machine that could be sold in vast numbers had stirred the imagination of many firms and most had come unstuck on it. It was to take the C50 step-through from Mr Honda to crack that nut.

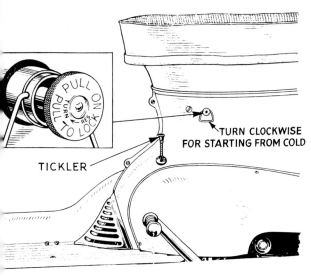

TICKLER

TURN CLOCKWISE
FOR STARTING FROM COLD

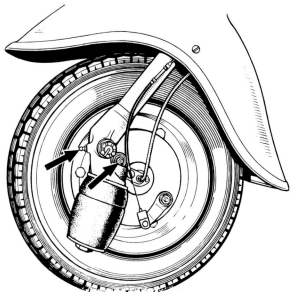

Above **Motorcycle orientated minor controls hardly endeared the Tina to the housewife**

Right above **Trailing arm front suspension with rubber spring medium. Note speedometer drive cable from hub centre**

Left **Both sides of the Tina, kickstart pedal on left, footbrake could be worked by either toe**

For all that, the new baby Triumph was a real attempt to design an easily operated machine for mass production. Why simple operation was considered so important is open to question as thousands of scooter riders were already coping happily with twistgrip gearchanges and the usual controls.

The new scooter was called the Tina and had twistgrip, brake lever and foot brake pedal only as the transmission was automatic. The brake pedal could be operated by either foot. Unfortunately the minor controls were still much in evidence and included a float tickler as well as an air control for cold starting.

The mechanical basis of the machine comprised the small two-stroke engine, the vee-belt transmission, the expanding pulleys which varied the ratio and the rear hub with its reduction gear. All these were assembled as a single unit to a beam built up from steel pressings welded together and this pivoted from the main frame to provide the rear suspension swinging arm. Although this did raise the unsprung weight it was an acceptable feature for a low speed scooter and kept the two belt pulleys at constant centres.

The engine was very straight-forward and based on dimensions of 50.4×50 mm which gave the horizontal, single cast iron cylinder a capacity of 99.75 cc. The inlet stub was on the left side with the small Amal complete with air cleaner clipped directly to it. Bolted to its underside was the exhaust system with a primary chamber feeding into a tubular silencer on the right. The cylinder head was in light alloy and the two ring piston gave a compression ratio of $7.0:1$.

The crankcase was split vertically on the cylinder centre line and supported the crank-

24   BSA GROUP SUPPLEMENT   MOTOR CYCLE   3 NOVEMBER 1966

TWO WAYS TO BEAT

Skip
through them on a
Triumph Tiger Cub

Snarled-up traffic, tempers on edge, people in a hurry getting nowhere. That's when the 200 cc Triumph Tiger Cub comes into its own. It'll skip through the city hold-ups without a care in the world. As for hard country cruising—it'll come back purring for more !

Specification includes high performance 200 cc O.H.V. engine with four-speed gearbox, separate chrome headlamp, valanced mudguards and de luxe dual seat. Finished in Pacific blue and white.

Its crisp performance, low running costs and absolute reliability make this model ideal for beginners and experienced rider alike.

Precision · Power · Performance

THOSE TRAFFIC JAMS

or Scoot
automatically through them on a Triumph T-10

The Triumph T-10. Learn to drive in minutes the AUTOMATIC way! No gears, no clutch: the Triumph T-10 automatic is always in the right gear—*automatically!*

PLUS THIS: ★Single cylinder two-stroke engine. ★Fully automatic variable drive. ★Pressed-steel back-bone type frame. ★Trailing link front suspension. ★Swinging arm rear suspension. ★Quickly detachable body and front panels. ★Interchangeable pressed-steel wheels.

The Triumph T-10—the only fully automatic scooter on the market—simple to ride and cheap to run.

And there are new two-tone paint finishes all lined up for 1967 T-10's—mimosa and ivory, and blue and ivory—in addition to the popular Ruby Amaranth.

See inside front cover for prices.

Triumph Engineering Co. Ltd., Meriden Works, Allesley, Coventry, England

Tigress and Tina

A late 1966 advert spread over two pages of *Motor Cycle* to push the Cub and the T10. The latter was out of place in a specialist magazine

shaft with a ball race on each side while the big end had a caged roller bearing. Four of the six bolts that held the case halves together also held the engine into its beam. On the right end of the crankshaft went a Wipac flywheel magneto with lighting coils and the rotor carried fan vanes. These were used in conjunction with a cowling which ran forward to partially enclose the head and barrel to give a degree of forced cooling.

The transmission went on the left with a pulley assembly on the crankshaft and another to the rear where it drove the wheel by a pair of enclosed helical gears. The front pulley contained the mechanism for altering the gear ratio and this was done by keeping the inner pulley flange fixed and moving the outer causing the vee-belt to change its working radius and hence altering the ratio.

The flange movement was governed by the engine speed. To do this a spider was splined to the crankshaft each of its three arms forming a radial track in which ran a large ball bearing. The outer pulley flange had matching tracks and was kept away from the inner by three light springs. As the engine speed rose centrifugal force threw the balls out and the two tracks were formed so that the outer flange was forced to move in.

When the engine idled the flanges moved far enough apart for the belt to clear them and lie on a ball bearing hub so no drive took place. To make sure this happy state continued until the rider was ready to move off it was arranged that the outer flange spring plate movement was linked to a pair of contracts. These were connected to the ignition via a start-and-drive switch so that while in 'start' any increase in engine speed closed the contacts and cut the ignition. Without this feature a blip of the throttle could have the scooter off down the road regardless of whether the rider was ready or not.

A Goodyear vee-belt connected the front pulley to the rear which had a spring loaded flange to help alter the gear ratio and to maintain the belt in its correct tension. The pulley shaft was cut with a helical pinion which drove the gear on the stub axle. The belt was guarded by a pressing behind and around it but no outer cover was used so it was open to the elements.

Between the pulleys and the belt runs protruded a pillion footrest, matched by another on the right just ahead of which went the kickstarter. Thus this was on the left and it moved in a forward direction for its quadrant to mesh with a pinion on the crankshaft.

The outcome of this design was that the engine was started and then the safety switch was turned to 'drive' after which opening the throttle caused the machinery to move off smoothly. When the desired speed was reached the throttle was eased to just maintain this. Closing the throttle disengaged the drive so there was no engine braking which was disconcerting if unexpected though not as much to those without experience of any vehicle.

The engine and transmission assembly were suspended from the main frame beam. This was built up with a long head stock welded to a box section beam that ran down, back and then up over the power unit. At the rear it was surmounted by a flat plate and under the beam went the pivot for the swinging arm assembly. This was controlled by a single spring and damper Girling unit on the left and the whole beam was part of the air intake. It did this with an intake grill at the front just below the bottom head race and a hose at the rear which connected to the air cleaner.

At the front the fork headstem was continued down on the left side of the wheel and at its lower end carried a pair of greased bushes. Pivoted in them was a cross-spindle formed in one with a single trailing arm which in turn carried the front wheel stub axle at its rear end. Just behind the pivot a second cross-spindle went through an eye bolt which hung down through a plate formed into the base of the fork leg. Below the plate went two rubber suspension bushes, one hard and one soft mix, while above it went a rebound buffer. A nut and a large washer on the end of the eye bolt completed the assembly which compressed the two main rubbers as the wheel rose to provide the front suspension.

Both brakes were 5 in. diameter drums with single leading shoes cable operated. At the front

The T10, was it the left side hand brake or the under-seat cut-out switch that caused the rider to walk away? Will he return and boot it into the handy canal lock?

the backplate was mounted onto the stub axle but at the rear it formed part of the reduction gearbox. The front drum had three wheel mounting studs fixed in it and the two ball races it turned on were pressed into its hub before the assembly went onto the stub axle. The hub drove the speedometer cable directly from a cap nut so the cable emerged from the left end of the axle to curl up to the speedometer via the inside of the headstem.

The rear drum fitted over the three studs and

was secured by a single screw and the wheel itself. Both wheels had pressed steel split rims and were fitted with 3·50 × 8 in. Avon tyres and had hub caps to conceal the wheel nuts.

Most of the body panels were pressed steel and built up into the usual scooter form with apron, footboard and engine enclosure. The front mudguard was however a pvc moulding. The petrol tank sat on the top of the rear panelling on the flat plate welded onto the top of the frame beam.

On top of the tank went the dual seat and the tank filler neck and cap projected through the rear of the seat. Fuel tap, air control and float tickler all protruded from the bodywork.

The speedometer was mounted in the centre of a pressing over the handlebars. Ahead of it went the light switch and behind it the safety switch. Throttle and front brake went on the right while the left bar carried a combined dipswitch, horn button and ignition cut-out. A 4 in. diameter Wipac headlamp was mounted in the front of the handlebar pressing and the finish was in lilac.

Once started and warmed up the machine was as easy to drive as claimed. Flick the switch over and open the throttle to go, shut off and brake to stop. As with the Tigress a range of accessories was listed including a screen, front carrier and bag hook.

At that the Tina continued unchanged until the middle of 1965 when it was revised and renamed the T10. This was mainly a cosmetic job as the mechanics stayed the same but the electrics differed in respect of the ignition and the safety switch. The first was modified to an external coil and the second item became automatic and worked by the weight of the rider on the seat. Until aboard, the switch kept the governor in circuit to cut the ignition as before if the engine speed rose.

The main change was the rear body which was lengthened and allowed to hinge about a point at the rear of the frame beam. In use it was held down by a toggle on each side at the front while the lower left side was detachable as a panel. The minor controls were moved to the front centre of the rear enclosure so they remained undisturbed when the main body was lifted.

Under the panelling an air cleaner was fitted to the far end of the intake hose connected to the carburettor. The brake controls were altered with the front lever going on the left handlebar and the rear pedal becoming a single one on the left side of the footboard centre section. At the front the suspension rubbers were hidden by a cover and the colour became flamboyant red.

Late in 1965 *Motor Cycle* tested the T10 and found it to work well in town and for commuting. It cruised at 40 mph, accelerated with the automatic transmission changing the drive ratio as it should and returned around 100 mpg. The fuel tank remained the same size at 1·5 gallon so could be refilled with a gallon of its mix of petrol and oil without risk of running dry. Unlike the Tina the filler cap went below the seat which hinged up for access. The machine's suspension was rather firm and the brakes worked well although the motorcycle tester found it disconcerting to have the front brake lever on the left.

The T10 was changed little for the rest of its life. In 1967 the weathershield panels were made detachable so each could be replaced by itself in the event of damage and for the same year two-tone colours options were made available. After that it was back to the original red and in that form it ran on to the middle of 1970 when it was dropped.

In that way the Triumph attempt to build scooters came to an end never having really become the success the factory had hoped for. Perhaps they were too well known by the public for their big twins to have been associated with a scooter, maybe they should have pushed it as a Sunbeam or even a New Hudson. Or maybe they were just too late for a fading market with products not to the public's choice.

4 | Trophy and Blazer

In 1958 the Tiger Cub was a well established model built in road and competition form with a swinging arm frame and still with its engine based firmly on the first Terrier design. That year it gave birth to a new model within the Group which preceded it in design with a central crankcase joint and this machine became the 250 cc unit construction C15 BSA.

The engine unit mirrored the Cub in most respects but from the first the crankcase split was on the cylinder centre. As with the Cub the head was light alloy and the barrel iron. The valve gear was the same with tappets side by side running directly in the crankcase. The pushrod tube was shorter as it sealed to the underside of the cylinder head and the rocker covers were screw caps, not lids.

Internally most detail design followed the Cub with a plain big end, plain timing side main bearing and skew drive to a points housing set in the crankcase top behind the barrel. Only with the oil pump did BSA differ as it had a gear unit driven by the ignition shaft.

Behind the engine and entirely contained in the right crankcase half went a four speed gearbox just like the Cub's and with exactly the same form of positive stop mechanism, selectors and camplate.

The power unit went into a frame with telescopic front and swinging fork rear suspension. Spoked wheels with full width drum brakes were fitted and the whole machine was typical of both

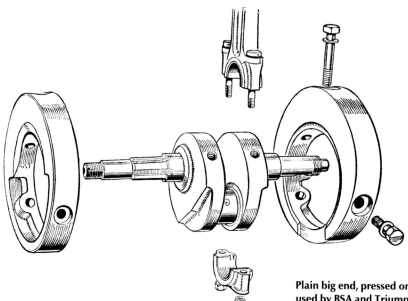

Plain big end, pressed on flywheels and forged crankshaft used by BSA and Triumph for their unit single from 1967

the period and the English industry at that time.

The C15 sold well and within a year it was joined by a pair of competition variants, modified to suit trials or scrambles use. Then in 1960 a larger version, the 350 cc B40, appeared and a year later a sports 250, the SS80, which had a roller big end.

All these models of what was still really an enlarged Cub continued for some years with minor alterations but the most noticeable change came in 1965. This was when the ignition points were set into the timing cover in the same way as had been done on the Cub for 1963.

For 1967 the C15 was replaced by the C25 Barracuda which had a well modified engine. Internally the crankshaft became a one piece forging but with two flywheel rings each pressed onto a web and secured by four bolts. It turned in ball and roller bearing mains and the split connecting rod was in light alloy with a plain big end. The crankcase was based on that used by the 440 cc BSA Victor engine and continued in the same form as before with the 4 speed gearbox built in unit.

On top of the crankcase went a light alloy barrel with iron liner and cooling fins were cast to a close pitch and to give a square look to the finished item. This style was continued up into the light alloy cylinder head and the two components completely enclosed the valve gear.

The engine unit went into a frame with single top and down tubes but with duplex ones under and behind it. Telescopic forks went onto the front with a swinging fork at the rear and both wheels had 7 in. drum brakes. The electrics were 12 volt and the machine was given a sporting appearance with a sculptured fibreglass fuel tank, narrow mudguards and a humped seat.

During 1968 the BSA became the B25 Starfire but before then was introduced under the Triumph label as the TR25W Trophy. In nearly every way it was the same machine with badge engineering but it was modified a little for trail use.

Changes in appearance were few. The rocker box side-plate and primary chaincase carried the Triumph name, the tank was in steel with the Meriden raised eyebrow style badges, the

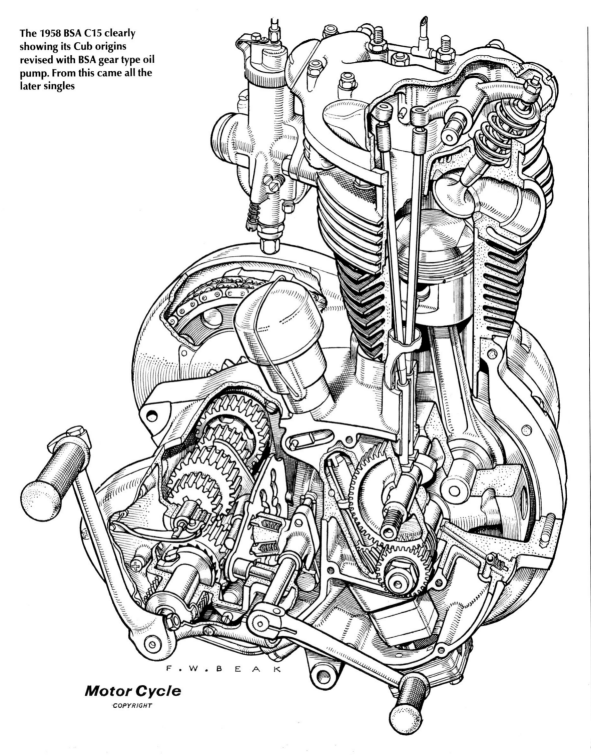

The 1958 BSA C15 clearly showing its Cub origins revised with BSA gear type oil pump. From this came all the later singles

F.W.BEAK

Motor Cycle
·COPYRIGHT·

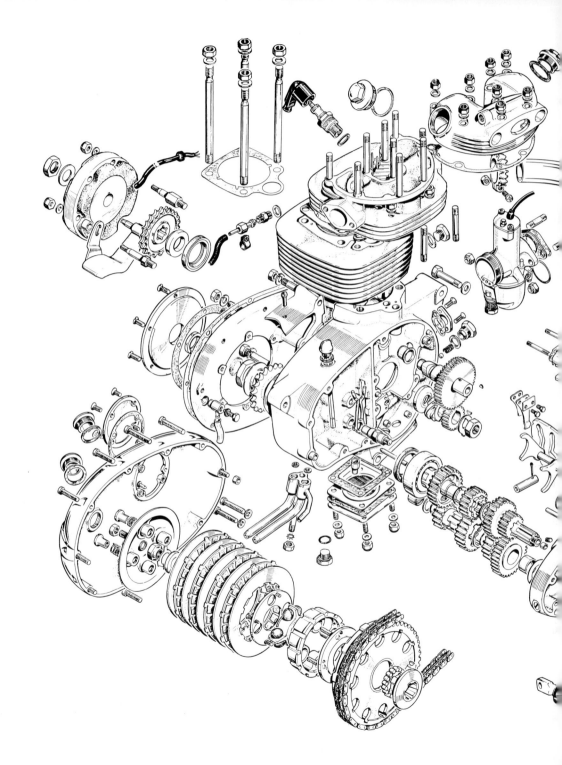

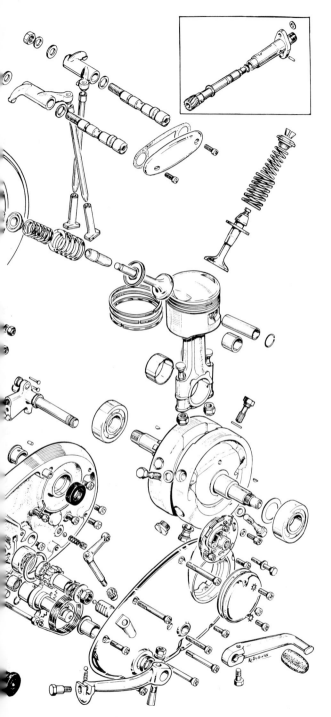

dualseat was ribbed and without a hump and the side covers were triangular and in black fibreglass with a flash. A grab rail went behind the seat and to suit the off-road use the gearing was lowered, the tyre sizes increased, a crankcase shield added, a smaller headlamp fitted and a high level exhaust with trials silencer installed. This ran on the right just above the timing case, curled inside the frame over the fork pivot and thus reached the silencer.

The engine and gearbox were the stock BSA complete with 10:1 compression ratio and eccentric rocker spindles for the valve clearance adjustment. The frame was the BSA while the forks were from the Tiger 90 model, the postwar 350 cc sports twin not the prewar 500 cc single. Single leading shoe drum brakes went into each wheel and for trail use the front tyre was 3·25 × 19 in. and the rear 4·00 × 18 in.

The result was a top speed just under 80 mph, good acceleration spoilt by an embarrassingly noisy silencer, fuel consumption around the 70 mpg mark and acceptable steering. The ride was tall in the saddle with the 8 in. ground clearance forcing the seat height up to 32 in. To match this, high rise handlebars were fitted and gave a comfortable position.

By late 1968 the new 250 had replaced the Cub from which it had grown and for 1969 it received a few alterations. At the front went a twin leading shoe brake, as used by a number of other models in both the BSA and Triumph ranges, and to be noted for a tendency to a spongy action. This arose due to the layout of the main cam lever and its connections to both the operating cable and the link to the second lever.

The exhaust pipe no longer tucked inside the frame but ran back in a straighter line from the top of the timing case to a longer silencer. This carried a chrome plated wire heat shield to pro-

The BSA C25 Barracuda engine in full detail as also used for the Triumph TR25W Trophy

tect the passenger's leg. The tank badge was new and had lost the grille appearance of the previous year and the colour was now given as hi-fi scarlet. Wheel and tyre sizes would seem to have been optional as although the handbook indicates 18 in. wheels front and rear, the machine illustrated retains its 19 in. at the front.

1970 brought a further change to the exhaust system which was moved to the left side and fitted with a new heat shield. At the same time an oil pressure switch was fitted to the engine with a warning light in the headlamp shell, the carburettor was rubber mounted and a smaller ignition coil adopted. In this form the model ran on until late in the year when it was replaced by two new ones shown at a massive group range launch.

The new models were the T25SS Blazer SS Street Scrambler and the T25T Trail Blazer Trail Bike, both of 250 cc and with much in common. The engine unit was the same in both and taken from the earlier model. It retained the same

Above **Drive side of the 1968 TR25W, badge engineered from the BSA**

Right **The 1968 timing side with tucked in exhaust pipe**

working dimensions, compression ratio and valve timing while the construction remained as before.

The engine was an all-alloy unit with an iron liner in the barrel which continued with the square style fins. The cylinder head was alloy with valve seat inserts and carried each of the two valves in a well in its upper surface. Duplex springs were used and a single casting covered them and carried the rockers on eccentric spindles. Small caps gave access to the area around the valve tip and rocker end so the gap could be measured and a plate on the side of the head was removable to allow this to be adjusted.

The three ring piston was held by a hollow gudgeon pin to the light alloy connecting rod. The rod had a split big end fitted with shell bearings and this worked on a forged crankshaft with bolted on flywheel weights. A ball race supported the timing side and a roller the drive in a vertically split crankcase which also housed the gearbox in the right half.

The timing gear was as simple as the first Terrier with the camshaft driven from the crankshaft by a gear pair, tappets working in the crankcase and pushrods set within the barrel and head tunnel. The camshaft drove the ignition cam and its auto-advance while a skew gear behind the crankshaft timing pinion drove the gear oil pump for the dry sump system.

Primary drive was on the left by duplex chain to the 4 speed, direct top gearbox. The clutch embodied a shock absorber and the final drive chain went on the left. An alternator went in the primary chaincase and ignition was by coil with the facility of being able to work with either a

flat battery or without a battery in circuit at all.

This engine unit was used by both BSA and Triumph and fitted into a frame common to both marques as were nearly all the cycle parts. The frame was unusual in that it also acted as the oil tank. It was fabricated from large diameter top and down tubes which were joined by duplex ones that ran under the engine and up to the seat nose. A sub-frame went to the rear to support the seat and rear fork units.

The front down tube was the main oil tank and was filled through an orifice in the top tube. A feed was taken from the base of the down tube into which a filter was fitted and this feed went to the engine. The return line had a take-off to supply the rockers and went via an external filter unit before returning to the headstock area.

The frame was based on the works moto-cross unit and carried the rear fork on needle roller bearings. The rear chain adjustment was also the pivot point which could be moved fore and aft and was located by a series of holes in a camplate

on each end of the pivot spindle. At the front the telescopic forks were new and turned in taper roller bearings. The forks were common to many of the two marque ranges and featured internal springs, exposed stanchions without protective gaiters and alloy sliders with caps secured by four studs.

The wheels and tyres varied for the two models but all used a new group design of conical hub at front and rear. For the Street Scrambler an 8 in. twin leading shoe drum went at the front and this had an airscoop cast into the backplate and was operated by a balanced cable working two very short cam levers. This hub went into a spoked wheel fitted with a 3·25 × 18 in. tyre.

The Trail Bike had a larger 3·00 × 20 in. front tyre but a smaller 6 in. diameter brake with single leading shoe action. At the rear the old type of quickly detachable hub was replaced by a conical one that lost the qd facility—a retrograde

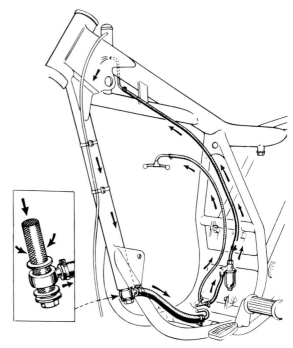

Above **T25SS Blazer of 1971, the T25T was much the same except for a smaller front brake, tyres and gearing**

Left above **For 1969 the exhaust ran outside the frame, the silencer was bigger and a twin leading shoe front brake was fitted**

Left **The frame for 1971 with oil carried in the down tube, note oil filter**

Strange twin silencers fitted to the single exhaust pipe of the TR5MX Avenger

step. In the hub went a 7 in. diameter single leading shoe drum brake and it was spoked to an 18 in. rim which carried a 3·50 in. tyre for the SS model and a 4·00 in. for the trail bike.

The remainder of the cycle parts were trail bike orientated and the most noticeable feature was the silencer which was a black lump that ran from the upswept pipe on the right along the line of the sub-frame to a high level exit. A perforated heat shield protected the rider.

Much of the electrical equipment was mounted in a single sub-assembly under the petrol tank and the machines were fitted with turn indicators and small headlamps. Control was by a light switch in the headlamp shell and poor, clumsy Lucas switches in units on each handlebar end.

As a trail machine the 250 cc Triumph was well liked for its ability to deal successfully with most off-road situations. For more serious use, or for trail riding at its best, a few changes were agreed as useful. Trials handlebars, a single seat, no lights and no battery were the main points while a 7:1 piston would not have knocked too much off the top end and would have made the engine more flexible.

But all such ideas were soon to be swept away for the group was in serious financial trouble. The

Triumphs were really BSAs with different badges and as the mighty Small Heath empire tottered and crashed they were among the many dragged down with the sinking ship. For them the end came in the Autumn of 1971 and they were no more.

So it seemed to be the end of the line for Triumph singles as the Meriden plant struggled to keep going. Its future became a political issue and in 1973 the NVT group appeared. Late that year the closure of the works was announced and this precipitated the long eighteen month sit-in by the work force.

During this period some machines were built at Small Heath and among them was the biggest Triumph single to continue the line for a short while. The model was the TR5MX Avenger but in truth it was a BSA B50MX with a few minor changes.

The engine unit was the final outcome of stretching the C15 to dimensions of 84 × 90 mm and 499 cc. It followed the same detail design in most areas, the major exception being the crankshaft which was built up with a caged roller big end. An extra ball race supported the shaft on the drive side and ignition was by a points controlled capacitor into a coil with the power coming from the alternator via a rectifier. A lighting kit was available as an extra but as no battery was used the system was not legal for road use in many states in the USA, the machine's prime market.

The primary drive ratio differed from that of the 250 and its oil was supplied from the engine via the mains to a weir set level, any surplus returned to the sump for collection by the scavenge pump. This returned the oil direct to the tank without any filter as on the smaller model with its plain big end.

The chassis was that of the trail 250 with oil in the frame and all the other features. One addition was a valve lifter to help starting and as before the chassis was fitted with a prop stand, sump plate and nice alloy fuel tank with yellow side panels and Triumph transfers.

The oddest and most noticeable feature of the machine was the exhaust. The pipe curled along on the right as usual, went behind the rear frame tubes but then connected to not one but two silencers mounted one above the other. The reason was to deal with the single large bangs a 500 puts out which was more of a problem than a twin of the same capacity. While it may have looked strange it did pull the noise level down to 88 db which was very acceptable.

For those who could accommodate more noise and wanted even more low down punch there was a big bore kit. This took the barrel out to 89 mm to make the capacity 560 cc and made the machine even more of a tree-stump puller. The noise was greater but still the low frequency bang of a 4 stroke single and so much less annoying than a 2 stroke buzz.

It was the last of a dying breed of machines that covered the trails in their own special way, thumping along without need to change gear most of the time. With the decline of the factory and the failure of BSA it could not carry on as a production model although such machines continued to be built in England by men such as Eric Cheney and Alan Clews, the latter producing a monster 608 cc banger at one time.

In time the trail single re-appeared, built by Yamaha, Honda and Suzuki, but never in quite the same easy riding form. Long before then the end had come for Triumph singles.

5 | Competition

The record of Triumph singles in competition goes back a long way to the earliest days of the company. Even before the one lap race at Brooklands there had been the TT and two years earlier, in 1905, the renowned Ixion, celebrated columnist of *The Motor Cycle* for so many years, was party to a Triumph test. Ixion, in real life the Rev. Basil H. Davies, undertook to ride 200 miles a day for six days and succeeded at the second attempt.

Such tests were popular in the early days and in 1910 Albert Catt managed 300 miles per day for the working week riding a belt drive with hub clutch. He had hoped to cover 2000 miles in all but engine trouble prevented this but did not interfere with the 300 per day average. The next year he did another run and pushed the figure to 400 per day and over 2400 in the week.

Another popular run was the Lands End to John O'Groats one and Ivan B. Hart Davies took his $3\frac{1}{2}$ hp Triumph over the 880 miles in 33 hr 22 mins in 1909, reducing the time to 29 hr 12 mins in 1911.

The Triumph singles had the honour of opening the first TT in 1907 when Frank Hulbert and Jack Marshall pushed off from the start. Behind them came the Collier brothers and it was Charles who won with the Triumphs 2nd and 3rd, Marshall having lost time dealing with a puncture. He made up for this the next year though when he won and set the fastest lap. This was to be the firm's one victory in the TT racing clas-

Jack Marshall at the end of his winning ride in the 1908 TT when he took the single cylinder class and set the fastest lap. He had been second in 1907

ses although in much later years they had several successes in production racing. In between those times they have a good number of near misses and many leader-board places.

In 1908 they were 3rd, 4th, 5th, 7th and 10th in the single cylinder class so really did pack the front of the field but in 1909 their best place was 3rd. That year only five of their machines finished and nine retired but the next they repeated their 3rd place and had all eight machines finish in good positions. In 1911 they lapsed a little but in 1912 were back in 2nd with other good places.

That was it in the pre-first-war era but they

Above **Ivan B. Hart-Davies at Lands End in 1909 having secured the record for the 886 miles trip from John O'Groats in 33 hours 22 minutes. He took over four hours off this in 1911**

Right **The Triumph team for the 1934 Senior TT comprising, from the left, Tommy Spann, Jock West and Ernie Thomas. The machine is Spann's, all three riders retired**

returned to the Island in 1921 with the new Ricardo model and a trio of side valve machines. It was one of the latter which recorded the fastest lap and another was 5th but in 1922 the Ricardo came good and ran home 2nd, Walter Brandish being the rider. He was much fancied to win in 1923 but crashed in practice at the bend that now bears his name. That was perhaps their best chance and their TT attempts gradually faded. They were 4th in 1924 and 3rd in 1927 but by then much of their competition success was gained at Brooklands by Vic Horsman.

At that oval concrete track in Surrey Vic won many events and raised the classic hour record several times with a distance of 86·52 miles in 1923 and 90·79 miles in 1925, the first time a 500 cc machine had broken the 90 mile barrier for a full sixty minutes. Years later, in 1937, Freddie Clarke used a well modified Tiger 80 to set the all time 350 cc Brooklands lap record at 105·97 mph. Clarke was also involved in an attempt for the Maudes Trophy that year, this being a cup awarded for the best demonstration of the touring facets of a machine. They had won it in 1933 and for 1937 ran three Tigers, one of each size, first at Donington Park and then at

Above left **Percy Tait racing a Cub at Mallory Park in March 1959; he finished second in the wet**

Left **D. Guy in the 1962 TT; he was still running when flagged off after five laps, that year only seven finished**

Above **Mrs Molly Briggs riding a Tiger 70 in the 1955 Scottish Six Days; she retired on the Tuesday**

Brooklands. They took the trophy and won it again in 1939 using a pair of twins.

The firm returned to the TT in 1934 with a team riding the Page-designed 500 cc single but struck a number of teething troubles. Although they all retired their work paved the way to the 5/10 having some success in private hands in later years although a single 1935 TT entry retired. It was 1947 before they had any success again in the Isle of Man and that came in the Clubman's TT. In the big class the Triumphs were twins but in the 250 cc event a prewar single ridden by Bill McVeigh led from start to finish. Unfortunately,

on examination, his Tiger 70 was found to have been rebored and was a touch over the capacity limit so he was excluded from the results. The problem of rebores, very real in 1947, had been raised back in March and it had been stated that an allowance would be given to cover this difficulty. In the light of this McVeigh appealed, and in August the exclusion was declared null and void so Triumph regained their first place.

For 1948 Bill moved on to the Senior Clubman's with a twin but another 250 cc single finished 3rd in its class. After that it was the twins which drew the publicity but years later, in 1962,

a Triumph single appeared again on the Manx circuit. This was in the 250 cc TT and the machine a well modified Cub ridden by D. Guy. He was only able to complete five of the six laps before being flagged off but at least his machine was still running and only seven others completed the distance that year.

The Cub became involved in club racing the next year with a new club being formed to run events for them. This was a limited success as the standard Cub capacity of 200 cc did not fit the normal class limits and the maximum to which it would open up seemed to be about

Left **John Giles aviates his Cub during a 1959 scramble**

Below **Another year, another meeting. Scott Ellis at the Gloucester Grand National in 1962**

Above **At the start of the 1959 British Experts Roy Peplow tries the throttle on John Giles' Cub**

Right above **Tiger Cub used by Artie Ratcliffe**

Right **Hard working Cub driven by Epsom dealer Arthur Wheeler in the 1960 Mitcham Vase**

Left **Artie Ratcliffe in the 1957 British Experts trial in which he was fourth**

Right **Johnny Giles in the Kickham trial in 1961**

230 cc. This still gave away size and the engine was inclined to protest about the combination of capacity and tuning. Also club riders found the Cub more expensive to prepare than the contemporary Bantam so most turned to the latter and relatively few Cub races were held.

Off road it was a different story and the postwar singles inherited a prewar history of competition in trials and the ISDT. Marjorie Cottle rode a Tiger 70 in the last two prewar years including the curtailed 1939 event while in 1936 the factory gained three golds using one of each size of the Tiger model.

Postwar the works team became Jim Alves and Peter Hammond riding the 350 cc twin with the former winning the first trials riders' star in 1950. In 1954 it was Alves who was the first to run a Terrier in a national trial, the St David's held in January and his machine was based on the standard model. A 21 in. wheel went into the front forks and competition tyres on both rims with slim alloy mudguards to shield them. The silencer was upswept and items such as lights and electric horn discarded to make a neat machine.

From then on more and more small Triumphs began to appear in trials at all levels. At first they were restricted by a lack of width in the rear frame which prevented a 4·00 in. section tyre being fitted but the more enterprising soon got round that obstacle. The energy transfer ignition did nothing to help the machine either and in those days before electronic ignition posed more of a problem.

Above **Specially prepared competition Cub with non-standard oil tank, tucked in exhaust and alloy tank**

Left **Gordon Farley in a 1964 trial**

In 1957 Roy Peplow began to ride the Cub along with Johnny Giles and that year Artie Ratcliffe won the tough Scott trail on one. 1959 was a good year for the team and never more so than in the Scottish Six Days which Peplow won following Ratcliffe's 3rd the year before. Peplow himself was 3rd in 1961 while Ray Sayer took that place in 1963. In 1965 the works team of Peplow, Sayer and Gordon Farley took the maker's team award despite Farley being involved in a collision with a car which shortened the Cub's wheelbase.

Don Smith on a Cheetah fitted with a Cub engine in a 1968 event. Note disc front brake

As the 1960 period ran on the factory went back to its 350 cc for a while but in the end the Cub itself was dropped and the group ran a team of BSAs derived from the C15, itself based on the Cub.

Right at the end, when only the road Cub was left, the sporting dealer firm of Comerfords in Thames Ditton, Surrey, bought a batch of Mountain Cubs and reworked them a little to produce a neat trials machine. Supplies curtailed the numbers but those that rode them liked them and they acted as a rearguard to the onslaught of the many Spanish trials machines that came in the later part of that decade.

While the Cub never attained the competition history of some other makes and models it did provide a light machine on which budding riders could cut their teeth. More than that, the off road models allowed many a rider to follow the sport at weekends while using the machine to commute during the week. It worked well at that and so carved its niche in history.

Appendix

Specifications

Model	2H, 2HC, T70	3S, 3SC, 3SE, 3SW	3H, 3HW	T80
Year from	1937 1	1937 2	1937 3	1937
Year to	1940 4	1940 5	1940 6	1940
Bore (mm)	63	70	70	70
Stroke (mm)	80	89	89	89
Capacity (cc)	249	343	343	343
Compression ratio (to 1)	6·92 7	5·3	6·7 8	7·5
Valve position	ohv	sv	ohv	ohv
inlet opens BTDC	47·5	19	47·5	47·5
inlet closes ABDC	68·5	60	68·5	68·5
exhaust opens BBDC	69·5	67	69·5	69·5
exhaust closes ATDC	46·5	29	46·5	46·5
Valve clear. (cold) in. (in.)	nil	0·004	nil	nil
Valve clear (cold) ex. (in.)	nil	0·007	nil	nil
Ignition timing (in.)	0·375	0·312	0·375	0·375
Points gap (in.)	0·012	0·012	0·012	0·012
Front tyre (in.)	3·25 × 19 9	3·25 × 19	3·25 × 19	3·00 × 20
Rear tyre (in.)	3·25 × 19	3·25 × 19	3·25 × 19	3·25 × 19
Brake front dia. (in.)	7	7	7	7
Brake rear dia. (in.)	7	7	7	7
Front suspension	girder	girder	girder	girder
Rear type	rigid	rigid	rigid	rigid
Petrol tank (Imp. gal)	3·25	3·25	3·25	3·25
Oil tank (Imp. pint)	6	6	6	6
Ignition system	magneto 10	magneto 11	magneto	magneto
Generator type	dynamo	dynamo	dynamo	dynamo
Output (Watts)	35	35	35	35
Battery (Volt)	6	6	6	6
Wheelbase (in.)	52·5	52·5	52·5	52·5
Ground clear. (in.)	6	6	6	6
Seat height (in.)	28·5	28·5	28·5	28·5
Width (in.)	28·5	28·5	28·5	28·5
Length (in.)	82	82	82	82
Dry weight (lb)	318 12	316	322	320

Model	2H, 2HC, T70	3S, 3SC, 3SE, 3SW	3H, 3HW	T80
Year from	**1937 1**	**1937 2**	**1937 3**	**1937**
Year to	**1940 4**	**1940 5**	**1940 6**	**1940**
Power: bhp	13 **13**	12	17	20
@ rpm	5200 **13**	4800	5200	5700

1 2HC—1938 **2** 3SC—1938, 3SE—1939, 3SW—1940 **3** 3HW—1940 **4** 2HC—1939 **5** 3SC—1938
6 3HW—1945 **7** T70—7·7 **8** 6·3 with flat top piston **9** T70—3·00 × 20 **10** 2HC—coil **11** 3SC—coil
12 T70—316 **13** T70—16/5800.

Model	5S, 5SE, 5SW	5H	T90	6S
Year from	**1939 1**	**1937**	**1937**	**1937**
Year to	**1940**	**1939**	**1938**	**1940**
Bore (mm)	84	84	84	84
Stroke (mm)	89	89	89	108
Capacity (cc)	493	493	493	599
Compression ratio (to 1)	5·6	6·1	7·68	5·6
Valve position	sv	ohv	ohv	sv
inlet opens BTDC	19	26·5	26·5	19
inlet closes ABDC	60	62·5	62·5	60
exhaust opens BBDC	67	75·5	75·5	67
exhaust closes ATDC	29	20·5	20·5	29
Valve clear. (cold) in. (in.)	0·004	nil	nil	0·004
Valve clear. (cold) ex. (in.)	0·007	nil	nil	0·007
Ignition timing (in.)	0·312	0·375	0·375	0·312
Points gap (in.)	0·012	0·012	0·012	0·012
Front tyre (in.)	3·25 × 19	3·25 × 19	3·00 × 20	3·25 × 19
Rear tyre (in.)	3·25 × 19	3·50 × 19	3·50 × 19	3·50 × 19
Brake front dia. (in.)	7	7	7	7
Brake rear dia. (in.)	7	7	7	7
Front suspension	girder	girder	girder	girder
Rear type	rigid	rigid	rigid	rigid
Petrol tank (Imp. gal)	3·25	3·25	3·25	3·25
Oil tank (Imp. pint)	6	6	6	6
Ignition system	magneto	magneto	magneto	magneto
Generator type	dynamo	dynamo	dynamo	dynamo
Output (Watts)	35	35	35	35
Battery (Volt)	6	6	6	6
Wheelbase (in.)	52·5	54	54	55
Ground clear. (in.)	6	6	6	6
Seat height (in.)	28·5	29·5	29·5	29·5
Width (in.)	28·5	28·5	28·5	28·5
Length (in.)	82	84	84	84

Model	5S, 5SE, 5SW	5H	T90	6S
Year from	**1939** **1**	**1937**	**1937**	**1937**
Year to	**1940**	**1939**	**1938**	**1940**
Dry weight (lb)	322	362	362	356
Power: bhp	15	23	28	18
@ rpm	4800	5000	5800	4800

1 5SE, 5SW—1940

Model	T15	T20	T20 Bantam Cub	T20 Super Cub
Year from	**1953**	**1954**	**1966**	**1967**
Year to	**1956**	**1965**	**1969**	**1969**
Bore (mm)	57	63	63	63
Stroke (mm)	58·5	64	64	64
Capacity (cc)	149·3	199·5	199·5	199·5
Compression ratio (to 1)	7·0	7·0	7·0	7·0
Valve position	ohv	ohv	ohv	ohv
inlet opens BTDC	30	30	30	30
inlet closes ABDC	50	50	50	50
exhaust opens BBDC	55	55	55	55
exhaust closes ATDC	25	25	25	25
Valve clear. (cold) in. (in.)	0·010	0·010	0·010	0·010
Valve clear. (cold) ex. (in.)	0·010	0·010	0·010	0·010
Ignition timing degree	8 retard	8 retard **1**	4	4
Front tyre (in.)	2·75 × 19	3·00 × 19 **2**	3·00 × 18	3·00 × 18
Rear tyre (in.)	2·75 × 19	3·00 × 19 **2**	3·00 × 18	3·00 × 18
Brake front dia. (in.)	5·5	5·5	5·5	5·5
Brake front width (in.)	1	1	1	1
Brake rear dia. (in.)	5·5	5·5	5·5	5·5
Brake rear width (in.)	1	1	1	1
Front suspension	teles	teles	teles	teles
Rear type	plunger	plunger **3**	s/a	s/a
Petrol tank (Imp. gal)	2·62	2·62 **4**	3	3
Oil tank (Imp. pint)	2·25 **5**	2·25 **5**	4	4
Box capacity (Imp. pint)	0·33	0·33		
Chaincase (Imp. pint)	0·50	0·50 **6**		
Ignition system	coil	coil	coil	coil
Generator type	alternator	alternator	alternator	alternator
Output (Watts)	54	55	60	60
Battery (Volt)	6	6	6	6
Wheelbase (in.)	49	49	51·5	51·5
Ground clear. (in.)	5	5 **7**	5·5	5·5
Seat height (in.)	28·2	30 **8**	30	31
Width (in.)	25	25		27·7
Length (in.)	77	77		79·4
Dry weight (lb)	175 **9**	182 **10**	218	220

Model	T15	T20	T20 Bantam Cub	T20 Super Cub
Year from	**1953**	**1954**	**1966**	**1967**
Year to	**1956**	**1965**	**1969**	**1969**
Power: bhp	8·3 **11**	10	10	10
@ rpm	6500 **11**	6000	6000	6000

1 1956—4   **2** 1956—3·25 × 16, 1960—3·25 × 17   **3** 1957—s/a   **4** 1956—3·0   **5** 1956—2·75   **6** 1960—0·33   **7** 1956—4, 1960—5   **8** 1956—28·5, 1957—30·5, 1960—29   **9** 1955—185   **10** 1955—195, 1956—205, 1957—215, 1960—220, 1962—215   **11** 1954—8/6000

Model	T20C	T20S	T20T	T20S/L
Year from	**1957**	**1959**	**1961**	**1961**
Year to	**1959**	**1961**	**1961**	**1961**
Bore (mm)	63	63	63	63
Stroke (mm)	64	64	64	64
Capacity (cc)	199·5	199·5	199·5	199·5
Compression ratio (to 1)	7·0	7·0	7·0	9·0
Valve position	ohv	ohv	ohv	ohv
inlet opens BTDC	30	30	30	39
inlet closes ABDC	50	50	50	61
exhaust opens BBDC	55	55	55	65
exhaust closes ATDC	25	25	25	35
Valve clear. (cold) in. (in.)	0·010	0·010	0·010	0·002
Valve clear. (cold) ex. (in.)	0·010	0·010	0·010	0·004
Ignition timing degree	4	8	8	16
Front tyre (in.)	3·00 × 19	3·00 × 19	3·00 × 19	3·00 × 19
Rear tyre (in.)	3·50 × 18	3·50 × 18	3·50 × 18	3·50 × 18
Brake front dia. (in.)	5·5	5·5	5·5	5·5
Brake front width (in.)	1	1	1	1
Brake rear dia. (in.)	5·5	5·5	5·5	5·5
Brake rear width (in.)	1	1	1	1
Front suspension	teles	teles	teles	teles
Rear type	s/a	s/a	s/a	s/a
Petrol tank (Imp. gal)	2·62	2·62	2·62	2·62
Oil tank (Imp. pint)	2·75	2·75	2·75	2·75
Box capacity (Imp. pint)	0·33	0·33	0·33	0·33
Chaincase (Imp. pint)	0·50	0·33	0·33	0·33
Ignition system	coil	ET	ET	ET
Generator type	alternator	alternator	alternator	alternator
Output (Watts)	55			
Battery (Volt)	6			
Wheelbase (in.)	49	49	49	49
Ground clear. (in.)	6·5		6	6
Seat height (in.)	30·5	30	30	30
Width (in.)	25		25	25
Length (in.)	77		77	77

Model	T20C	T20S	T20T	T20S/L
Year from	**1957**	**1959**	**1961**	**1961**
Year to	**1959**	**1961**	**1961**	**1961**
Dry weight (lb)	205	210	210	210
Power: bhp	10	10	10	14·5
@ rpm	6000	6000	6000	6500

Model	T20S/S	T20S/H	TR20	TS20
Year from	**1962**	**1962**	**1962**	**1962**
Year to	**1965**	**1966**	**1965**	**1963**
Bore (mm)	63	63	63	63
Stroke (mm)	64	64	64	64
Capacity (cc)	199·5	199·5	199·5	199·5
Compression ratio (to 1)	9·0	9·0	7·0	9·0
Valve position	ohv	ohv	ohv	ohv
inlet opens BTDC	39	39	30	39
inlet closes ABDC	61	61	50	61
exhaust opens BBDC	65	65	55	65
exhaust closes ATDC	35	35	25	35
Valve clear. (cold) in. (in.)	0·002	0·002	0·010	0·002
Valve clear. (cold) ex. (in.)	0·004	0·004	0·010	0·004
Ignition timing degree	16	16	8	16
Front tyre (in.)	3·00 × 19	3·00 × 19	2·75 × 21	2·75 × 21
Rear tyre (in.)	3·50 × 18	3·50 × 18	4·00 × 18	3·50 × 19
Brake front dia. (in.)	5·5	5·5	5·5	5·5
Brake front width (in.)	1	1	1	1
Brake rear dia. (in.)	5·5	5·5	5·5	5·5
Brake rear width (in.)	1	1	1	1
Front suspension	teles	teles	teles	teles
Rear type	s/a	s/a	s/a	s/a
Petrol tank (Imp. gal)	2·62	3·0	2·62	2·62
Oil tank (Imp. pint)	2·75	2·75	2·75	2·75
Ignition system	ET	coil	ET	ET
Generator type	alternator	alternator	alternator	alternator
Battery (Volt)		6		
Wheelbase (in.)	49	49	49	49
Ground clear. (in.)	6	6	9	9
Seat height (in.)	30	30	30	30
Width (in.)	25	26	31	31
Length (in.)	77	77	77	77
Dry weight (lb)	223	230 **1**	210 **2**	200 **3**
Power: bhp	14·5	14·5	12	14·5
@ rpm	6500	6500	6000	6500

1 1963—223   **2** 1963—212   **3** 1963—208

Model	TS1	Tina	T10
Year from	**1958**	**1962**	**1965**
Year to	**1965**	**1965**	**1970**
Bore (mm)	61·5	50·4	50·4
Stroke (mm)	58	50	50
Capacity (cc)	172	99·75	99·75
Compression ratio (to 1)	7·5 **1**	7·0	7·0
Ignition timing (in.)	0·062 **2**	0·125	0·093
Points gap (in.)	0·018	0·018	0·018
Tyre (in.)	3·50 × 10	3·50 × 8	3·50 × 8
Brake front dia. (in.)	5	5	5
Brake front width (in.)	1		
Brake rear dia. (in.)	5	5	5
Brake rear width (in.)	1		
Front suspension	teles	trailing arm	trailing arm
Rear type	s/a	s/a	s/a
Petrol tank (Imp. gal)	1·5	1·5	1·5
Box capacity (cc)	125		
Chaincase (cc)	250		
Rear chaincase (cc)	120		
Rear hub (cc)		50	50
Ignition system	magneto	magneto	magneto
Generator type	alternator		
Battery (Volt)	6		
Wheelbase (in.)	48	46·4	46·4
Ground clear. (in.)	5	5	
Seat height (in.)	28	26	28
Width (in.)	24	24	24
Length (in.)	72	63·5	68·5
Dry weight (lb)	236	143	150
Power: bhp	7·5	4·5	4·5
@ rpm	5000	5000	5000

1 1959—6·5, mid 1960 from engine S6001—7·6 (factory list figures)　**2** 1960 with 7·6:1 cr—0·156

Model	TR25W	T25SS	T25T	TR5MX
Year from	**1968**	**1970**	**1970**	**1974**
Year to	**1970**	**1971**	**1971**	
Bore (mm)	67	67	67	84 **1**
Stroke (mm)	70	70	70	90
Capacity (cc)	247	247	247	499 **1**
Compression ratio (to 1)	10	10	10	9 or 10·5
Valve position	ohv	ohv	ohv	ohv
inlet opens BTDC	51	51	51	
inlet closes ABDC	68	68	68	
exhaust opens BBDC	78	78	78	
exhaust closes ATDC	37	37	37	
Valve clear. (cold) in. (in.)	0·008	0·008	0·008	
Valve clear. (cold) ex. (in.)	0·010	0·010	0·010	
Ignition timing degree	37	37	37	
Points gap (in.)	0·015	0·015	0·015	
Front tyre (in.)	3·25 × 18 **2**	3·25 × 18	3·00 × 20	3·00 × 21
Rear tyre (in.)	4·00 × 18	3·50 × 18	4·00 × 18	4·00 × 18
Brake front dia. (in.)	7 **3**	8 (2 LS)	6	6
Brake rear dia. (in.)	7	7	7	7
Front suspension	teles	teles	teles	teles
Rear type	s/a	s/a	s/a	s/a
Petrol tank (Imp. gal)	3	2	2	2
Oil tank (Imp. pint)	4	4	4	4
Box capacity (Imp. pint)	0·5	0·5	0·5	0·5
Chaincase (Imp. pint)	0·25	0·25	0·25	
Ignition system	coil	coil	coil	capacitor
Generator type	alternator	alternator	alternator	alternator
Output (Watts)	110	110	110	
Battery (Volt)	12	12	12	
Wheelbase (in.)	53	54	54	55·5
Ground clear. (in.)	8	7	8	7·5
Seat height (in.)	32	32	32	32
Width (in.)	27	29	29	
Length (in.)	83	85	85	
Dry weight (lb)	315	290	287	
Power: bhp	24	22·5	22·5	24
@ rpm	8000	8250	8250	6000

1 Big bore kit—89 mm/560 cc   **2** or 3·25 × 19   **3** 1969—2LS

Transmission

To avoid repetition of data and notes the gearbox types and ratios are set out below followed by a list of sprockets, top gear ratio and gearbox fitted to each model, year by year. From this the intermediate ratios may be calculated.

Except for the scooters all models used chain transmission and prewar the primary was $\frac{1}{2} \times \frac{5}{16}$ in. and the final $\frac{5}{8} \times \frac{3}{8}$ in. All Terrier and Cub models had $\frac{1}{2} \times \frac{3}{16}$ in. final chain but the primary varied. All Terrier engines and Cubs to engine 17388 built at the end of the 1955 season had $\frac{3}{8} \times \frac{7}{32}$ in. primary chain. From engine 17389, 1956 season so built about September 1955, the T20 and new T20C used $\frac{1}{2} \times \frac{3}{16}$ in. chain up to engine 35846 built at the end of the 1957 season. From engine 35847 all engines were fitted with a $\frac{3}{8}$ in. duplex primary chain. All the unit construction models of 250 and 500 cc had $\frac{3}{8}$ in. duplex primary and $\frac{5}{8} \times \frac{1}{4}$ in. final chains.

On the scooters the Tigress had gear primary and a $\frac{3}{8}$ in. duplex final chain. The primary of the Tina and T10 was by vee-belt with a variable ratio which with a reduction drive by helical gears in the rear hub gave an overall reduction that varied from 5:1 to 14·75:1.

Optional sprockets were available for the Cub with the gearbox ranging from 13 to 18 teeth for engines up to number 35846 and from 13 to 19 for engines after that number which used the neoprene oil seal. For all models rear wheel sprockets were available with 46, 48, 50, 52, 54, 56 or 58 teeth. The 47 tooth BSA Bantam sprocket could be re-drilled to fit and became Cub listing from 1965.

Gearbox type	Internal ratios			
Prewar	1·0,	1·20,	1·73,	2·53
T15 and T20 standard	1·0,	1·316,	2·06,	2·99
T20 wide	1·0,	1·459,	2·271,	3·282
T20 close	1·0,	1·20,	1·875,	2·725
T20 extra close	1·0,	1·194,	1·558,	2·058
TS1	1·0,	1·28,	2·05,	2·99
Unit 250 and 500	1·0,	1·244,	1·646,	2·652

Model	Year	Sprockets				Top ratio	Gearbox
		E	C	G	W		
2H, 2HC, T70	1937–40	18	43	18	46	6·105	Prewar
3S, 3SC, 3SE, 3SW	1937–40	18	43	18	46	6·105	Prewar
3H, T80	1937–40	20	43	18	46	5·494	Prewar
3HW	1940–45	19	43	18	46	5·784	Prewar
5S, 5SE, 5SW	1939–40	20	43	20	46	4·945	Prewar
5H, T90, 6S	1937–40	23	43	18	46	4·778	Prewar
T15	1953–56	19	48	17	48	7·133	Std.
T20	1954–55	19	48	18	48	6·737	Std.
	1956–57	18	36	17	54	6·353	Std.
	1958–59	19	48	18	46	6·456	Std.
	1960–65	19	48	17	46	6·836	Std.
	1965–66	19	48	17	47	6·984	Std.
T20C	1956–57	18	36	16	54	6·750	Std.
	1958–59	19	48	16	46	7·263	Std.

Model	Year	Sprockets				Top ratio	Gearbox
		E	C	G	W		
T20S	1959–60	19	48	17	54	8·025	Wide
T20T	1960–61	19	48	16	54	8·526	Wide
T20S/L	1960–61	19	48	17	48	7·133	Close
T20S/S	1961–62	19	48	17	48	7·133	Close
T20S/H	1962–66	19	48	17	48	7·133	Close
TR20	1962–66	19	48	16	58	9·158	Wide
TS20	1962–64	19	48	16	58	9·158	Ex. close
T20S/C	1966–68	19	48	17	47	6·984	Std.
TS1	1958–60	45	102	19	38	4·533	TS1
	1961–65	45	102	18	39	4·911	TS1
TR25W	1968–70	23	52	15	52	7·838	Unit
option	1968–70	23	52	15	49	7·386	Unit
T25SS	1970–71	23	52	17	52	6·916	Unit
T25T	1970–71	23	52	16	52	7·348	Unit
TR5MX	1974	28	52	14	52	6·898	Unit

Colours

Triumph Terrier and Tiger Cub Colours

These have been laid out by year, market and model. The production year ran from August or September to July or August and not from January to December. UK colours were also those used for general export.

The main colours are given first and abbreviated for the detail parts.

Abbreviations are :-

AB	-	Azure blue
AR	-	Amaranth red
AW	-	Alaskan white
AZ	-	Aztec red
Bl	-	Black
Bu	-	Burgundy
CB	-	Crystal blue
CG	-	Crystal grey
CP	-	Chrome plating
FF	-	Flamboyant flame
Fl	-	Flame
FR	-	Firecracker red (also known as Bushfire red)
FRR	-	Flamboyant ruby red
FS	-	Flamboyant scarlet (also known as Sapphire red)
GN	-	Green
Go	-	Gold
GR	-	Grenadier red
HS	-	Hi-fi scarlet
HY	-	Hunting yellow
Iv	-	Ivory
KB	-	Kingfisher blue
MB	-	Metallic blue
NB	-	Nutley blue (also known as Perivale blue)
PA	-	Polished alloy
PB	-	Pacific blue
Re	-	Red
RR	-	Ruby red
SB	-	Shell blue sheen
Si	-	Silver
SS	-	Silver sheen
Wh	-	White

Note that wheel rims were always chrome-plated but painted centres were only used for 1954-56. The T15 had amaranth red centres lined in gold and the T20 had shell blue sheen centres lined in black.

All other painted parts were in black, except for the T15 which used amaranth red, and the military models which were normally finished in army green or khaki, depending on the build contract.

From frame number 38130, built during 1958, the T20 and T20J had new tank badges fitted, other models retained the old type for the rest of the year. Note that the petrol tank colours for the 1959 T20S could be reversed. The colours for some models are not known and any data on these would be gratefully received by the author and the marque specialist.

Year	UK or USA	Models	Colours	Petrol tank upper/ lower	Mudguards main guard/ centre/ lining	Oil tank/ tool -box	Side panels	Front brake plate	Tank badge logo/ back
1954-1956	Both	T15	Amaranth red	AR	AR/-/-	AR	-	AR	Wh/AR
1954-1956	Both	T20	Shell blue sheen	SB	SB/Bl/Wh	Bl	-	SB	Wh/Bl
1957	Both	T20 T20C	Crystal grey	CG	CG/Bl/Wh	Bl	-	CG	Wh/Bl
1958	UK	T20 T20C	Crystal grey	CG	CG/Bl/Wh	Bl	-	CG	Wh/Bl
	USA	T20 T20J	Crystal grey or Aztec red	CG or AZ	CG/Bl/Wh AZ/Bl/Wh	Bl Bl	- -	CG Si	Wh/Bl Wh/Bl
		T20C T20CA	Crystal grey or Aztec red	CG or AZ	CG/Bl/Wh AZ/Bl/Wh	Bl Bl	- -	CG Si	Wh/Bl Wh/Bl
1959	UK	T20	Crystal grey	CG	CG/Bl/Wh	CG	CG	CG	Wh/Bl
		T20C	Crystal grey	CG	CG/Bl/Wh	Bl	-	CG	Wh/Bl
		T20S	Ivory & azure blue	Iv/AB	Iv/AB/Go	Bl	-	Bl	Wh/Bl
	USA	T20 T20J	Crystal grey or Aztec red	CG or AZ	CG/Bl/Wh AZ/Bl/Wh	CG	CG AZ	CG	Wh/Bl Wh/Bl
		T20C T20CA	Crystal grey or Aztec red	CG or AZ	CG/Bl/Wh AZ/Bl/Wh	Bl Bl	- -	CG	Wh/Bl Wh/Bl
		T20S	Ivory & azure blue or red & ivory	Iv/AB or Re/Iv	Iv/AB/Go Re/Iv/Go	Bl Bl	- -	Bl Bl	Wh/Bl Wh/Bl
1960	UK	T20	Crystal grey	CG	CG/Bl/Wh	CG	CG	CG	Wh/Bl
		T20S	Ivory & azure blue	Iv/AB	Iv/AB/Go	Bl	-	Bl	Wh/Bl
	USA	T20 T20J	Crystal grey or Aztec red	CG or AZ	CG/Bl/Wh AZ/Bl/Wh	CG	CG AZ	CG	Wh/Bl Wh/Bl
		T20S T20W	Ivory & azure blue	Iv/AB	Iv/AB/Go	Bl	-	Bl	Wh/Bl
1961	UK	T20	Silver sheen & black	Bl/SS	SS/Bl/Wh	SS	SS	SS	Wh/Bl
		T20S T20T	Ruby red & silver sheen	RR/SS	SS/RR/Go	Bl	-	SS	Wh/Bl
		T20SL	Ruby red & silver sheen	RR/SS	SS/RR/Go	Bl	-	SS	Wh/Bl
	USA	T20 T20J	Silver sheen & black	Bl/SS	SS/Bl/Wh	SS	SS	SS	Wh/Bl
		T20S T20T	Ruby red & silver sheen	RR/SS	SS/RR/Go	Bl	-	SS	Wh/Bl
		T20SL	Ruby red & silver sheen	RR/SS	SS/RR/Go	Bl	-	SS	Wh/Bl
1962	UK	T20	Silver sheen & black	Bl/SS	SS/Bl/Go	SS	SS	SS	Go/Bl
		T20SS T20SH	Burgundy & silver sheen	Bu/SS	SS/Bu/Go	Bl	-	SS	Wh/Bl
		TR20 TS20	Burgundy & silver sheen	Bu/SS	PA	Bl	-	SS	Wh/Bl
	USA	T20 T20SS	Flame & silver sheen	Fl/SS	SS/Fl/Go	SS	SS	SS	Go/Bl
		T20SC	Flamboyant ruby red & silver sheen	FRR/SS	SS/FRR/Go	Bl	-	Bl	Bl/Go
		T20SR	Flamboyant ruby red & silver sheen	FRR/SS	SS/FRR/Go	Bl	-	SS	Bl/Go
		TR20	Burgundy & silver sheen	Bu/SS	PA	Bl	-	SS	Wh/Bl

Year	UK or USA	Models	Colours	Petrol tank upper/ lower	Mudguards main guard/ centre/ lining	Oil tank/ tool -box	Side panels	Front brake plate	Tank badge logo/ back
1963	UK	T20	Flame & silver sheen	Fl/SS	SS/Fl/Go	Fl	SS	SS	Go/Bl
		T20SH	Burgundy & silver sheen	Bu/SS	SS/Bu/Go	Bl	-	SS	Go/Bl
		TR20 TS20	Burgundy & silver sheen	Bu/SS	PA	Bl	-	SS	Wh/Bl
		T20SS	Kingfisher blue & silver sheen	KB/SS	SS/KB/Go	Bl	-	SS	Wh/Bl
		T20WD							Wh/GN
	USA	T20	Flamboyant ruby red & silver sheen	FRR/SS	SS/FRR/Go	FRR	SS	SS	Go/Bl
		T20SS							
		T20SC	Flamboyant flame & silver sheen	FF/SS	SS/FF/Go	Bl	-	Bl	Bl/Go
		T20SR	Flamboyant flame & silver sheen	FF/SS	SS/FF/Go	Bl	-	SS	Bl/Go
		TR20 TS20	Burgundy & silver sheen	Bu/SS	PA	Bl	-	SS	Wh/Bl
1964	UK	T20	Hi-fi scarlet & silver sheen	HS/SS	SS/HS/Go	HS	SS	SS	Go/Bl
		T20SH	Hi-fi scarlet & silver sheen	HS/SS	SS/HS/Go	Bl	-	SS	Go/Bl
		TR20	Hi-fi scarlet & silver sheen	HS/SS	PA	Bl	-	SS	Wh/Bl
		T20SS	Kingfisher blue & silver sheen	KB/SS	SS/KB/Go or PA	Bl	-	SS	Wh/Bl
		T20WD							Wh/GN
	USA	T20	Flamboyant scarlet & silver sheen	FS/SS	SS/FS/Go	FS	SS	SS	Go/Bl
		T20SM	Crystal blue & silver sheen	CB/SS	PA	Bl	-	Bl	Bl/Bl
		T20SC	Kingfisher blue & silver sheen	KB/SS	PA	Bl	-	Bl	Bl/Bl
		T20SR	Kingfisher blue & silver sheen	KB/SS	PA	Bl	-	SS	Bl/Bl
1965	UK	T20 T20SH	as 1964						
		TR20 T20SS	as 1964						
		T20WD	as 1964						
		T20SM	Hunting yellow	HY	PA	Bl	-	Bl	Bl/Bl
	USA	T20	as 1964						
		T20SM	Hunting yellow	HY	PA	Bl	-	Bl	Bl/Bl
		T20SC	Hunting yellow	HY	PA	Bl	-	SS	Bl/Bl
		T20SR	Pacific blue & silver sheen	PB/SS	PA	Bl	-	SS	Bl/Bl

Year	UK or USA	Models	Colours	Petrol tank upper/ lower	Mudguards main guard/ centre/ lining	Oil tank/ tool -box	Side panels	Front brake plate	Tank badge logo/ back
1966	UK	Bantam Cub	Nutley blue & white	NB/Wh	Wh/Wh/Go	NB	-	Wh	NB/Wh
		T20SH	Metalic blue & Alaskan white	MB/AW	MB/AW/Go	MB	-	MB	MB/AW
		T20SM	Grenadier red & Alaskan white	GR/AW	PA	Bl	-	Si or Bl	AW/GR
	USA	T20SM T20M	Grenadier red & Alaskan white	GR/AW	PA	Bl	-	Si or Bl	AW/GR
1967	UK	Bantam Cub	as 1966	FR/CP	FR/Bl/Wh	FR	-	-	Bl/Go
		Super Cub	Firecracker red						
		T20SM T20M	as 1966						
		T20MWD							
	USA	T20SM T20M	as 1966						
1968	UK	Bantam Cub	as 1966						
		Super Cub	as 1967						
		T20SM T20M	as 1966						
		T20MWD	as 1967						
	USA	T20SM T20M	as 1966						
1969	UK	Bantam Cub	as 1966						
		Super Cub	as 1967						
		T20M	as 1966						
		T20MWD	as 1967						
1970	UK	T20M	as 1966						

Scooters

TS1
1958/60 Shell blue sheen.
1961 As 1958 with options in primrose or grey with ivory weathershield.
1962/65 As 1961 with mimosa option in place of primrose.

Tina
1962/65 Lilac.

T10
1965/66 Flamboyant red.
1967 As 1965, now called translucent ruby or ruby amaranth. Options in mimosa and ivory or blue and ivory.
1968/70 Flamboyant red, as 1965.

Unit singles

1968: TR25W
Flamboyant red, black frame and forks, black side covers with flash, chrome plated wheel rims and headlamp shell, Triumph 'eyebrow' tank badges.

1969/70: TR25W
As 1968 in hi-fi scarlet, new tank badge without grille section.

1970/71: T25SS, T25T
Black frame and exhaust, tank coloured with dark flash on each side and Triumph transfer.

Engine and frame numbers

1934

Model	Engine prefix	Model	Engine prefix
2/1	1R4	5/1	1S4
2/5	5R4	5/2	2S4
3/1	1T4	5/3	3S4
3/2	2T4	5/4	4S4
3/5	5T4	5/5	5S4
		5/10	10S4

Frame prefixes were SII for the 250 and 350 sv, SI for the 350 ohv and 500.

1935 and 1936

As 1934 except last number of prefix changed to '5' for 1935 and '6' for 1936. Plus:

Year	Model	Engine	Frame
1935	L2/1	1L5	L
1936	L2/1	1L6	L
	T70	T1L6	L
	T80	T2T6	SI
	T90	T5S6	SII

1937 to 1940

Sequence of year, model and number used for engine with year expressed as last digit only e.g. 7-3H-1264, 8-T80-3465 Frame prefix TL for 250 and 350, TH for 500

Terrier and Cub

Note that model season year normally ran from August or September to July or August. Machines left the factory with matching engine and frame numbers.

Year	Starting number	Models			
1954	101	T15	T20		
1955	8518	T15	T20		
1956	17389	T15	T20		
1957	26276	T20	T20C		
1958	35847	T20	T20C	T20J	T20CA
1959	45312	T20	T20C	T20J	T20CA
		T20S			
1960	56360	T20	T20S	T20J	T20W
1961	69517	T20	T20T	T20S/L	T20J
		T20S			
1962	81890	T20	T20S/S	T20S/H	TS20
		TR20	T20SC	T20SR	
1963	88347	T20	T20S/H	TR20	TS20
		T20SC	T20SR	T20SS	T20WD
1964	94600	T20	T20S/H	TR20	T20SC
		T20SR	T20SS	T20WD	T20SM
1965	99733 to 100013 101-	T20	T20S/H	TR20	T20SM
		T20SC	T20SR	T20SS	T20WD
1966	101	T20 (Bantam Cub)	T20M	T20S/H	
		T20SM			
1967		T20 (Bantam Cub & Super Cub)			
		T20SM	T20M	T20MWD	
1968		T20 (Bantam Cub & Super Cub)			
		T20SM	T20M	T20MWD	
1969		T20 (Bantam Cub & Super Cub)			
		T20M	T20MWD		
1970	- 10050	T20M			

Mid-season changes of note:

1956	18596	crankpin end diameter increased
1960	57617	centre crankcase split
1961	78000	cast iron oil pump body
1962	84629	ball bearing mains, bigger big end

Engine and frame numbers from mid-1965 to 1970 ran from 101 to 10050 but in a random manner. The same number was used by different models. Refer to marque specialist for accurate dating.

Unit single

1968

Prefix TR25W, number from C101

1969–74

Code system using two letters for month and year followed by serial number and preceded by model type. Month code ABCDEGHJKNPX for January to December. Year code:

C August 1968 to July 1969   D August 1969 to July 1970
E August 1970 to July 1971   G August 1971 to July 1972
H August 1972 to July 1973   J August 1973 to July 1974

TS1 scooter

Year	Engine	Frame
1960	S101	4001
1961	S6720	18801B
1962	S11407	30140B
1963	S12498	31825B
1964	S13263	33661B
1965	S13576	34300B
last		34468

Carburettor settings

Model	Year	Type	Size	Main	Pilot	Slide	Needle Pos.	Needle Jet
147 Z	1933	74	$\frac{25}{32}$	70		4/5	1	
150 XO, XO5	1933–35	93	$\frac{5}{8}$	40M	30	2		
175 XO7/1	1934–35	TT	$\frac{3}{4}$	130		7	4	
175 XO7	1934–35	93	·656	45M	30	2		
250 WO	1933	74	$\frac{25}{32}$	75		4/4	1	
250 L2/1	1935–36	75	$\frac{13}{16}$	100		5/4	3	
250 2/1, 2/5	1934–36	75	$\frac{7}{8}$	110		5/3	3	
350 WL	1933	74	$\frac{25}{32}$	70		4/5	2	
350 3/1	1934–36	75	$\frac{7}{8}$	120		5/4	3	
350 3/2	1934–36	76	1	150		6/4	3	
350 3/5	1934–35	76	1	150		6/3	3	
500 Super B	1933	76	1	160		6/4	2	
500 SSB	1933	76	$1\frac{1}{16}$	200		6/4	2	
500 Super B	1933	89	$1\frac{1}{8}$	200		29/3	3	
500 B, BS	1934–35	89	$1\frac{1}{8}$	200		29/3	3	
500 5/1, 5/3	1934–36	76	1	150		6/4	3	
500 5/2, 5/4, 5/5	1934–36	89	$1\frac{1}{8}$	200		29/3	3	
500 5/10	1935–36	TT	$1\frac{3}{16}$	400		5	4	
550 A	1933	75	$\frac{7}{8}$	110		5/5	3	
250 2H, T70	1937	75	$\frac{7}{8}$	110		5/2	2	
250 2H, T70	1938–39	75	$\frac{7}{8}$	120		5/4	3	
350 3H	1937–38	76	1	150		6/3	2	
350 3H	1939	76	1	150		6/4	2	
350 3HW	1940–45	276	1	150		6/4	2	
350 3S	1937–39	75	$\frac{7}{8}$	120		5/4	3	
350 T80	1937	76	1	150		6/3	2	
350 T80	1938–39	76	1	160		6/4	3	
500 5S	1939	75	$\frac{7}{8}$	120		5/4	3	
500 5H, T90	1937–39	89	$1\frac{1}{8}$	200		29/3	1	
600 6S	1937–39	76	$1\frac{1}{16}$	170		6/5	3	

Model	Year	Type	Size	Main	Pilot	Slide	Needle Pos.	Needle Jet
T15	1953	332	$\frac{3}{4}$	120		4	2	·086
T15	1954–56	332	$\frac{11}{16}$	90	20	4	3	·086
T20, T20J	1954–57	332	$\frac{3}{4}$	100	20	4	3	·086
T20 export	1959	332	$\frac{13}{16}$	140	15	4	3	·086
T20	1962–66	32	$\frac{11}{16}$	85	15	2	2	·104
T20 export	1962–65	32	$\frac{11}{16}$	110	15	2	2	·103
T20S/C	1967	375	$\frac{25}{32}$	90	25	$3\frac{1}{2}$	3	·105
T20S/C	1968	622	22 mm	120	25	3	2	·105
T20C	1957	332	$\frac{3}{4}$	100	20	4	3	·086
T20S	1959–60	376	$\frac{15}{16}$	140	20	3	3	·106
T20S/L	1961	376	$\frac{15}{16}$	140	20	3	3	·106
T20T	1960–61	375	$\frac{25}{32}$	100	25	$3\frac{1}{2}$	3	·105
T20S/S	1962	376	$\frac{15}{16}$	140	20	$2\frac{1}{2}$	3	·106
T20S/H	1962–66	376	$\frac{15}{16}$	140	20	$2\frac{1}{2}$	3	·106
TS20	1962–64	376	$\frac{15}{16}$	140	20	$2\frac{1}{2}$	3	·106
TR20 and WD	1962–66	375	$\frac{25}{32}$	100	25	$3\frac{1}{2}$	3	·105
T20SM	1965–67	376	$\frac{15}{16}$	140	15	$3\frac{1}{2}$	3	·105
TS1	1959–60	363	$\frac{13}{16}$	130	15	$3\frac{1}{2}$	5	·106
TS1	1961–65	363	$\frac{13}{16}$	130	15	3	3	·106
Tina	1962	32	$\frac{23}{32}$	115	25	2	3	·105
Tina	1962–65	32	$\frac{23}{32}$	105	25	2	3	·105
T10	1965–68	32	$\frac{23}{32}$	95	15	4	2	·105
T10	1967–70	32	$\frac{23}{32}$	95	15	4	3	·105
TR25W	1968	928	28 mm	160		3	1	·106
TR25W	1969–70	928	28 mm	200		$3\frac{1}{2}$	1	·106
T25SS, T25T	1970–71	928	28 mm	200		$3\frac{1}{2}$	1	·106
TR5MX	1974	932	32 mm	180		$3\frac{1}{2}$	3	·106

Zenith					Slow run	Starter		
T20, T20C	1958–59	17MX	17 mm	78	50	200/65		
T20, T20T	1960–61	18MX	18 mm	84	45	200/65		

Prices

The UK prices of the machines of the postwar period are set out below and included in them is the purchase tax payable.

Date	T15	T20	T20C	T20S	T20T	T20S/L
6.11.52	£125 4s. 6d.					
29.10.53	£117 12s. 0d.	£127 4s. 0d.				
27.10.55	£121 4s. 0d.	£131 8s. 0d.				
25.10.56		£143 16s. 10d.	£150 0s. 10d.			
24.10.57		£149 14s. 0d.	£155 18s. 9d.			
15.10.59		£144 15s. 0d.		£159 4s. 6d.		
6.10.60	**T20S/S**	£148 7s. 5d.			£161 12s. 9d.	£164 1s. 0d.
19.10.61	£169 18s. 6d.	£153 19s. 6d.	**T20S/H**	**TR20**	**TS20**	
14. 2.62			£174 16s. 8d.	£185 5s. 2d.	£180 7s. 0d.	
24.10.62		£166 4s. 0d.	£188 8s. 0d.	£199 16s. 0d.	£194 8s. 0d.	
10.10.64		£170 15s. 11d.	£188 14s. 3d.	£200 1s. 2d.		
2. 9.65		£165 0s. 3d.	£179 3s. 2d.	£190 0s. 2d.		
5.11.66	**T20S/C**	£167 14s. 0d.				
1.12.66	£184 2s. 1d.					

Terrier and Cub accessories were as below.

	T15 dualseat	Pillion rests	Prop stand	Lock	Rev-counter
29.10.53	£2 2s. 0d.	19s. 3d.			
2. 9.54	£2 2s. 0d.	19s. 3d.	18s. 8d.		
25.10.56		19s. 11d.	19s. 3d.		
24.10.57		£1 0s. 0d.	19s. 4d.	13s. 4d.	
15.10.59		19s. 4d.	18s. 9d.	12s. 8d.	
6.10.60		19s. 11d.	19s. 11d.	13s. 3d.	
19.10.61		£1 2s. 1d.	£1 2s. 9d.	15s. 4d.	
24.10.62		£1 4s. 0d.	£1 4s. 8d.	16s. 3d.	£7 16s. 0d.
2. 9.65		£1 7s. 6d.	£1 8s. 9d.	18s. 10d.	£9 0s. 3d.
5.11.66		£1 7s. 11d.	£1 9s. 3d.	19s. 2d.	

Scooters

	TS1	Tina	T10
30.10.58	£164 19s. 8d.		
14. 4.60	£159 10s. 7d.		
19.10.61	£162 5s. 1d.		
29. 3.62		£93. 9s. 0d.	
24.10.62	£152 17s. 0d.	£94 10s. 0d.	
10.10.64	£152 17s. 0d.	£99 15s. 0d.	
2. 9.65			£109 4s. 0d.
3.11.66			£121 13s. 0d.

Scooter accessories for TS1 at 20.10.60

screen	£4 19s. 6d.	spare wheel	£5 9s. 0d.
rear carrier	£3 15s. 6d.	spare wheel cover	£1 12s. 6d.
front carrier	£3 10s. 0d.	pannier frames, each	£1 17s. 6d.
wheel discs, each	£1 14s. 6d.	pannier bags, each	£2 11s. 1d.

Model recognition points With commencing engine numbers where applicable.

These notes are to some extent a precis of the main text and should be used in conjunction with it and the other appendices.

1953
T15
Plunger frame, gear indicator, roller big end, greased forks, Lucas electrics, 2.75 in. tyres.

1954
T15
Coil behind gearbox, rectifier under seat, gear indicator added, optional dualseat and pillion rests. Flywheel sludge trap added (4859).
T20
Larger capacity on **T15** lines, raised exhaust system, **T15** type system available as option, dualseat, 3.00 in. tyres, 80 mph speedometer, plain big end (3905), raised gearing. Ribbed mudguards.
Mid Year
The T15 was fitted with the plain big end.
T15 and T20
Forged centre stand (6670), increased clutch leverage (8165), heavy duty clutch cable and adjuster added to pressure plate (5360).

1955
T15
Snap connections to switch, higher charge rate, rectifier diameter reduced from 4.5 to 2.75 in., prop stand option, auxiliary balls in oil pump.

1956
T15
Larger oil tank, bonded clutch segments, stiffer petrol tank, more upswept bars, deeper chainguard, legshield option.
T20
As **T15**, larger petrol tank, 3.25 x 16 in. tyres, modified frame, raised gearing, coil under seat with plastic sheet shield, engine with stiffer big end, heavier flywheels, $\frac{1}{2}$ in. pitch primary chain, altered chaincase, filler screw aligned with clutch centre.
Late in year **T15** stopped.

1957
T20
s/a frame, Girlings, new seat, damped forks, rear brake torque stay, deeper chainguard, butted rear spokes, oil tank froth tower, rocker box fins, heavy duty main and big end coating, larger crankpin spigot, special tolerance primary chain.
T20C
New model as **T20**, trials tyres, narrow mudguards, lower gearing, upswept exhaust, Trophy style silencer, bigger wheels, butted front spokes, stronger fork yoke, fork leg bridge, crankcase shield, longer prop stand, no centre stand.

1958
T20
Duplex primary chain, deeper chaincase, cast iron clutch drum, new gearbox sprocket form and garter seal, lock socket on headstock with optional lock, new silencer, deeper rear mudguard, new tank badge (38130).
T20J
Junior model for USA with power restricted to 5 bhp by carburettor modification, otherwise as **T20**.
T20C
Transmission changes and lock socket as **T20**, front fork gaiters.
T20CA
USA variant of **T20C** with low-level exhaust and road tyres
From mid-year Zenith carburettor for all models (39167).

1959
T20C
New cylinder barrel, deeper fins, hidden fixing studs, more robust base, crankcase cut away more for bigger sprocket, double gearbox seal.
T20
As **T20C** plus partial enclosure panels, oil tank and toolbox moved back, repositioned oil tank cap, new petrol tank of deeper section.
T20S
New model much as **T20C**, engine as **T20**, energy transfer ignition, direct lighting, small headlamp shell with two push switches, D speedometer, no battery fitted, heavy duty forks as on **350** cc twin, no nacelle, gaitered forks, rear fork able to take 4 in. tyre, lowered gearing, wide ratio gearbox, crankcase shield, front mudguard stay altered.

Late in year **T20C** and **T20CA** stopped.

1960

T20
17 in. wheels, muted silencer, modified cylinder with exhaust port moved, larger inlet valve, 18 mm Zenith, gearing changed, less chaincase oil.

T20S
As 1959

T20W
USA road version of later **T20T** with lights, very few sold.

Later in year from engine 57617, new crankcase castings with split line on cylinder centre, same internals, new distributor clamp screw, shorter barrel studs.

1961

T20
New oil pump, oil feed to skew gears.

T20T
New model much as **T20S**, wide ratio gearbox, toolbox under seat, oil pump as **T20**, stop light coils in alternator, crankcase shield.

T20S/L
New model much as **T20S**, close ratio gearbox, details as **T20T**, higher compression ratio, sports camshaft, Monobloc, more power, rev-counter option which if used calls for round speedometer head.

Late in year **T20T**, **T20S**, **T20J** and **T20S/L** stopped.

1962

T20
Amal for some export markets, better oil pump with cast iron body, larger tail light with integral reflector, no separate reflector, new fuel tap.

T20S/S
New model based on **T20S/L** with 1962 **T20** features, crankcase shield, optional low compression engine.

T20S/H
New model, two piece crankpin, ball race timing main, pressed in timing mainshaft, skew and timing gears separate, increased oil flow, coil ignition, no crankcase shield, ribbed front tyre, switches under seat, single central headlamp dipswitch, close-ratio gears.

TR20
New trials model, engine type as **T20S/H**, low compression ratio, energy transfer ignition, wide gear ratios, short seat, strenghtened footrests and rear unit lower pivot, footrests and pedal moved to rear, barrel silencer, one piece chainguard, exhaust pipe inside rear frame stay, alloy mudguards.

TS20
New scrambles model, **T20S/H** engine, energy transfer ignition, close gear ratios, short seat, strengthened as **TR20** details, open exhaust inside rear frame stay, alloy mudguards.

T20SC
USA model with high-compression piston, sports cam, Monobloc, trials tyres, upswept exhaust, standard gears.

T20SR
USA road model as **T20SC** but having road tyres, low exhaust, close-ratio gears.

During year new crankcase with timing side ballrace main bearing for all models (84269).

1963

All models
Contact points in timing cover, clutch cable access hole in cover, finned rocker box lids.

T20S/H
Gear position plunger in crankcase, oil tank drain plug, miniature rectifier, rev-counter option.

T20
As **T20S/H** except for rev-counter, two switches in nacelle, new speedometer.

TR20, TS20, T20SS, T20SC, T20SR
No other changes.

T20WD
Based on **T20T** with lights, speedometer, dualseat, centre stand.

Late in year **TS20** stopped.

1964

All models
Solid crankpin, aluminium bronze skew gear for oil pump drive, reshaped clutch shock absorber rubbers.

T20
Combined horn button and dipswitch, no central rib for rear mudguard, bolt-on handlebar levers.

T20S/H
As **T20** plus extended rear chainguard shielding lower chain run.

TR20, T20SS, T20WD, T20SR, T20SC
No other changes.

T20SM
USA model with wide-ratio gears, trials tyres, low-

compression piston, sports cam, ET ignition, lights.

1965

T20

No gear indicator.

T20S/H

No gear indicator, longer cranked kickstart pedal, new front fork for all sports models.

Late in year **T20SS, T20SC, T20SR, TR20, T20WD** stopped.

1966

All models

Sliding block oil pump fitted, roller big end.

Bantam Cub

Bantam frame, forks, separate headlamp shell, oil tank to match BSA type centre panels, 18 in. wheels, oil pump as above, square head and barrel, roller big end.

During year **T20S/H** stopped.

T20M

USA model similar to **T20SM.**

1967

Super Cub

Super Cub as 1966 **Bantam Cub** with full width hubs, Bantan tank, revised front mudguard mounting, improved silencer.

Bantam Cub, T20SM, T20M

No changes.

T20MWD

Military model with standard piston and cam, wide-ratio gears, dualseat, lights.

1968

All 1967 models unchanged.

TS20M stopped in year.

1969

No changes to existing models.

Bantam Cub, Super Cub, T20MWD stopped production.

1970

T20M unchanged, production ceased.

Scooters

1958

TS1

Introduced with 175 cc engine based on BSA Bantam, 4 speeds, stub axle wheels, 3·50 × 10 in. tyres.

1959

TS1

No change other than compression ratio.

1960

TS1

Compression ratio raised in mid-year.

1961

TS1

Gearing altered.

1962

TS1

No changes.

Tina

Introduced with 100 cc engine, automatic vee-belt transmission, rubber front suspension, 3·50 × 8 in. tyres.

1963/64

TS1, Tina

No changes.

1965

TS1

No change, stopped mid-year.

Tina

No change, revised in mid-year to

T10

New version of **Tina**, same mechanics, hinged seat, seat safety switch, hinged rear body, front brake lever on left, single rear brake pedal, cover on suspension rubber.

1966

T10

No changes.

1967

T10

Weathershield panels detachable.

1968/70

T10

No changes, stopped mid-year, 1970.

Unit singles

1968

TR25W

Introduced, based on BSA 250 cc engine unit, trail format, upswept exhaust on right tucked behind frame.

1969

TR25W

Exhaust pipe not tucked in, longer silencer with heat shield, twin leading shoe front brake, 18 or 19 in. front wheel.

1970
TR25W
Exhaust system on left, oil pressure switch, oil light in headlamp shell, rubber mounted carburettor, smaller ignition coil.
Late in year model stopped and replaced by
T25SS
Same engine, new frame carrying oil in down tube, chain adjuster at rear fork pivot, no front fork gaiters, conical hubs, upswept exhaust on right, lozenge silencer with heat shield, 8 in. twin leading shoe front brake.
T25T
As **T25SS** except 6 in. single leading shoe front brake, different tyres and gearing.

1971
T25SS, T25T
As 1970, stopped in Autumn.

Model charts

Single cylinder Triumphs 1953–1974

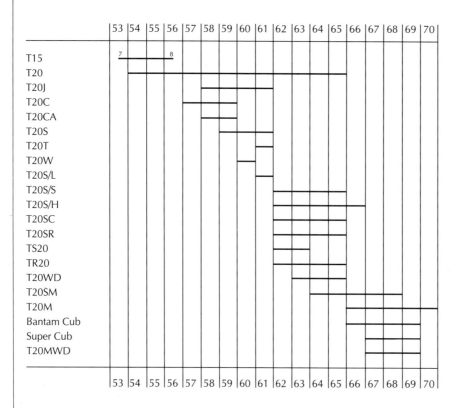

Pre-Second War Triumphs 1934–1940

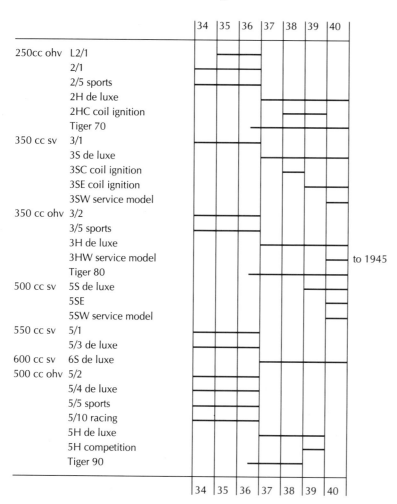

		34	35	36	37	38	39	40
250cc ohv	L2/1							
	2/1							
	2/5 sports							
	2H de luxe							
	2HC coil ignition							
	Tiger 70							
350 cc sv	3/1							
	3S de luxe							
	3SC coil ignition							
	3SE coil ignition							
	3SW service model							
350 cc ohv	3/2							
	3/5 sports							
	3H de luxe							
	3HW service model							to 1945
	Tiger 80							
500 cc sv	5S de luxe							
	5SE							
	5SW service model							
550 cc sv	5/1							
	5/3 de luxe							
600 cc sv	6S de luxe							
500 cc ohv	5/2							
	5/4 de luxe							
	5/5 sports							
	5/10 racing							
	5H de luxe							
	5H competition							
	Tiger 90							
		34	35	36	37	38	39	40